Go Figure

Go Figure

Humor, Adventure and Coincidence

*To Katie
Enjoy!!!
Renée*

Renée V. Stark

The author has tried to recreate events, locations, and conversations from her memories of them. In some instances, in order to maintain their anonymity, the author has changed the names of individuals and places. She may also have changed some identifying characteristics and details such as physical attributes, occupations, and places of residence.

Copyright © 2014 by Renée V. Stark

All rights reserved. No part of this book may be reproduced or transmitted in any form or by any means, electronic or mechanical, including photocopying, recording, or any information storage and retrieval system, without permission in writing from the author.

Author photograph by Marc Sidoux

ISBN: 978-0-615-92637-7

Printed in the United States of America by:
BOOKLOGIX
Alpharetta, Georgia

10 9 8 7 6 5 4 3 2   1 1 2 6 1 3

∞This paper meets the requirements of ANSI/NISO Z39.48-1992 (Permanence of Paper)

Contents

Acknowledgments	vii
Introduction	ix
Vacation Time at the New Jersey Shore	1
Courting in the North Country	7
A Trip to Hawaii	15
Sightseeing with the Kids	23
The Guests	29
Waiting for the Christmas Painting	35
Hindenburg	39
Waiting for the Plane	43
Life Is Buggy	47
The Presidents	51
Valerie Was My Sister	55
The Dancing Lady	59
The Orientals Next Door	63
Europe, Here We Come	67

Dinner with Whom?	77
The Spiritualist	81
Go to Alaska, Okay?	85
The Diner on 41	93
A Meeting at Wal-Mart	97
The Christmas Party	105
Trees are Great	111
Italy on the Horizon	115
What, the Ballet?	125
Cathy Returns to Italy	129
What Were the Questions?	137
The Fortuneteller	143
Moving Is Complicated	147
Architecturally Speaking	155
Annie Chang	159
One Day in the Life of a Cat Owner	165
Seoul, Korea, and Garlic	171
SLG Means Spiritual Living Group	179
Hi, George	185
Bingo Day at The Summit	189
A Borders Adventure	193
About the Author	199

Acknowledgments

A group called the Silvery Quill gave me the inspiration to write the stories you will find in this book.

Looking back at some of the occurrences that take place in life, you have to chuckle. The coincidences that seem to be happening daily almost go unnoticed.

I thank all the characters you will find in these stories. They all contributed in amazing ways.

Thanks to all that gave me encouragement and listened to me read these stories.

Thank you, Tom, for your suggestions and sharing your expertise.

Thanks also to the Spiritual Living Group; John and Mary Stegen; Barbara and Dick Howard; Pat and Brian Minkle; Norma and Bradley Chatfield; Silvery Quill; Jane Lewitinn; Judy Colbs; Mary Sabadosh; Lenda Cardullo; Pat and Barbara Burke; Joan and Dick Powers;

Val and Marti; Plantation North Book Club; Dr. Morris Miehl; Marvin and Sunny Newmark; Howard Miners for telling me to get rid of the unnecessary words; Alan Christ who was always ready to listen; David and Harriet Beckler for encouraging me to publish; and Carol Christie, my cheerleader.

My family, daughters, sons, Mom and Dad, granddaughters, grandsons, friends, coworkers, artists, neighbors, and fellow travelers are all contributors to this writing experience.

Lastly, my gratitude and love to my husband Tom Stark for encouraging me in the writing process.

Introduction

Who knew these stories would appear in a book?

After painting for fifty years, writing was thought about occasionally but never acted upon. The time had come, and the stories kept twirling around in my head.

This book is about life events, coincidences, looking at the bright side, laughter, and amazement.

Our journey through life takes twists and turns with lots of surprises. Sometimes thought-provoking happenings go by unnoticed. Looking back, you can see the humor and gain wisdom from the simplest memories.

I hope you will enjoy these stories as much as I have enjoyed writing them.

Vacation Time at the New Jersey Shore

Packing for four kids, two adults, and a German shepherd was not easy. Our vacation was to be spent at the Jersey Shore for two weeks. The girls did not want to go; they would miss their friends, there was nothing to do at the shore, and we would all be confined in a rental upstairs of a house. We would have a beautiful view of the beach and ocean, and the place fit all our needs. The boys would be okay; they would fly kites.

We packed the attitudes, and the dog was ready to go bye-bye in the car. We decided to take two separate cars. Our eldest daughter had just gotten her license, and she wanted to have a car available in case we wanted to go out. She could take the kids to get a burger. Little did we realize she would have her first minor accident in a

Burger King parking lot. Packing the car, it dawned on us how much stuff they thought they needed, and we realized it was a good idea to have two cars. There would be plenty of room, and I was tired of traveling with a German shepherd on my lap.

Tom took the two boys and one girl in his car, and I had the oldest with her ton of luggage and the dog. Laura drove to the shore, and I still managed to have the dog on my lap.

We lost sight of Tom somewhere along the way. When we arrived at Ship Bottom, I realized I did not have the address of our rental house. We drove up and down looking for Tom's car, and we couldn't find it anywhere. This was way before cell phones. Finally, Laura and I decided to get a cup of coffee at the diner and sit by the window and wait for a miracle. Tom went riding by; I flew out of the diner, and he was gone. Another ten minutes went by, he passed again, and this time he noticed our car parked with the German shepherd's head hanging out the window. We had never been happier to see him.

We all settled in to the apartment; the girls would room together and the boys together. Tom and I would share a room with the German shepherd. Mind you, no one was excited to visit the shore, but Tom and me. We love the ocean, the sound of the surf, the smell, walking along the shore with your feet digging into the hot sand, getting tan, laying on a blanket under an umbrella, and just mellowing out. As soon as we were settled, the children were arguing over who would walk the dog. I found this puzzling because not one of them ever volunteered to walk the dog. They all wound up walking the dog. They came home with the dog happily wagging her tail, all smiles on the children's faces; it seems they all fell in love on the walk. It was great to see smiles and enthusiasm. All four could not wait to get to the beach.

It was like they were the Pied Piper; out of nowhere were all these kids, just the right ages for our assortment of ages.

The shepherd was my dog and that created a problem for me. Every time I went to sit on the beach, the dog would go flying down to where I was, running and jumping across people lying on their blankets. Sand would fly everywhere, and very surprised people would yell and scream. She kept escaping the apartment somehow. We decided Tom would have to drive her home to our boarding place for the remainder of our vacation. The children had all the friends they needed, and no one was offering to walk the dog anymore anyway.

On rainy days, we'd tour the island or set up a puzzle, and the children wouldn't even mind the rain. They always found things to do on the beach. Every evening Tom would fix their kites and run up and down the beach. For the girls, miniature golf, soft ice cream, hamburgers, Cokes, music, and boys were the order of the day. The boys played football in the sand, played in the waves, built sand castles, collected shells, and generally had a wonderful time. All the kids had tanned brown as berries.

One morning we woke up and found the oldest boy was missing. We were beside ourselves. After missing him for an hour, in he walks with some fish. It seems he got up at five in the morning, walked to a nearby dock, and was fishing. That is a scare no one needs to have; imagine what we were imagining. He never did that again without permission, I can assure you. I cooked the fish for his breakfast, and he was a happy angler.

Laura made friends with a young surfer. He wore a black wetsuit with a zipper up the front. One evening, we were having rain with thunder and lightning. He was coming out of the ocean to take cover, and the lightning hit the zipper on his wet suit. He died on the way to the hospital. That was her first experience of the death of a friend. She was devastated.

The boys witnessed a much less devastating death on this trip. One day we bought a twenty-five-pound live lobster; the biggest lobster I had ever seen. Yes, we were going to eat him. We bought a galvanized garbage pail to cook him in. It took a long time to heat the water. After he was cooked and dead, we realized we had no way to crack his shell. We found two boards, put him between the boards, and slowly drove the car over the boards. That did the trick—the rest we managed with pliers and a hammer. We feasted royally. We even had lobster for breakfast. I must mention that lobster cost one dollar a pound at that time.

It was time for our two-week vacation to finally come to an end. The children were tense about leaving their friends. The boys were kind of cool about the situation, but the girls were hysterical. The younger daughter was never going to see "him" again (who knew which "him"). She was sobbing. I pointed out they could write and stay in touch by phone. ("Yes, but it won't be the same!") Both girls were quiet on the way home. They did not want to leave their boyfriends. It seems that was the situation in both directions. They hadn't wanted to go and now they didn't want to leave. Teenagers.

We picked up the dog from the kennel, and before we could get her in the car, she somehow wound up on the roof. She was crying and whining, looking miserable. That was the last time she ever went to a kennel. She obviously did not enjoy her stay there, and from then on she went everywhere with us. On the way home, she sat on my lap again. I became accustomed to being wrinkled, smelling doggy, and having a German shepherd sitting on my lap.

Go Figure…

Courting in the North Country

The girls decided no matter how cold it was, they were going to the game. Football games are big doings in Minnesota. It doesn't matter that there is ten feet of snow, it's below thirty-two degrees, and the stadium doesn't have a roof. (The new stadium had not been built at that time.)

Most people pack an elaborate lunch to be eaten out of the car trunk or truck trunk. The custom is called tailgating. Eating fried chicken seems to be the normal thing at these events. Tom and I were asked to attend the game and join the tailgating happening, and we said, "No way"; we would eat our fried chicken in the warmth of our lovely home and watch the game on TV.

The girls were driving to the stadium and skipping the tailgating thing since they didn't like freezing to death, and they were going alone.

Little did we know at the time there was a carload of men driving to the stadium from Rosholt, South Dakota. They were brothers and a few friends, five in all. They were faithful about going to the football games together.

Shortly after the game started, the girls decided they were freezing their butts off and needed refuge and maybe a few beers. The young men from Rosholt decided the same thing and went to the bar across from the stadium where the girls happened to be. They were also enjoying a few beers.

The men settled in a booth across from the girls. Laura kept looking at one of the young men, could not take her eyes off him. Lisa, the younger one, went over to the table when Laura went to the ladies' room and told the young man her sister thought he was cute. Would he like to join them? Laura was delighted when she returned. The girls had an opportunity to meet a carload of men, and fun was had by all, I guess, because the ballgame did not last until one a.m.

Sometime later, we learned only that his name was Dwight, and she would only say, "He was nice people."

We checked the map to find out where Rosholt was, and we had never met anyone from South Dakota. At the time, we rode a motorcycle and decided we would go to Rosholt on the bike to check out this young man. Tom's brother and sister-in-law rode their bike with us. We arrived in Rosholt, a little bitty town in the middle of nowhere. As we circled around the town, we had the feeling folks were looking out of their closed curtains to see who was in town on motorcycles. Later, I found that is exactly what they were doing.

We saw a young bearded man with long hair walking down the street. We stopped and asked if he knew Dwight, and he was Dwight. He asked how come we were in Rosholt, and we explained we were passing through on the way to North Dakota. No one passes through Rosholt by accident, and he knew we were looking him over. He passed our test and did, indeed, seem like good people.

Things progressed and we were hearing about wedding plans. Laura and Dwight were getting married in Rosholt in October, and we would not have to be concerned about the wedding because everyone in Rosholt was happy Dwight was finally marrying. Most of the girls in Rosholt did not pass the test, but the girl from the Cities did (Minneapolis and St. Paul are referred to as "the Cities"). Having originally come from the New York area is even a bigger deal.

The women from that small town knew how to put together a reception. The reception hall was in the center of town next to the bowling alley; the name bowling alley was correct. It contained one alley. They were digging the potatoes, picking the corn, killing the hogs, picking the string beans, serving the beef, baking the cake and bread. It sounded good to me. All I needed to do was address the place cards. My handwriting is lovely. Tom would pay for the music at the dance, to be held at the coliseum.

We were to host the wedding rehearsal dinner. We met Dwight's parents for the first time, and we found them delightful, really nice country folks. They were nervous to meet two folks from the Cities.

After the dinner, we went to the local bar, also in the center of town, where our guests from the Cities met us for drinks. Many of Dwight's friends joined us. Tom had asked the waitress to keep a running tab, as he would pick up the bar bill. He noticed she had filled up about ten pages of entries, and he asked how much the bill was so far. She said it was up to $20.00; it seems drinks were 35 cents, much to his amazement, and he suggested she keep the tab open all night.

The next day was beautiful, sunny, and bright as only South Dakota can be. The air was crisp and clean. What a wonderful day for a wedding. The wedding was to take place at eleven in the morning. It seemed a little early.

Laura's son Eric was not at all happy about this wedding. He had been the center of the universe for five whole years, and he did not want to share Mom with Dwight or move away from Grandma and Grandpa. Here he was, all dressed up and very uncomfortable in his clothes. I had told him he had to stay clean and neat until after the wedding. I would tell him when he could go wild.

Laura had never been prettier. Her dress was lovely, and she was running around in it for hours before the wedding. Dwight was running around with her. What happened to the old custom, you do not see the bride until she walks down the aisle?

Tom gave his little girl away again, and we were all teary eyed. When we were outside the church, Eric said, "Now, Grandma?"

"Yes, Eric. Now." He was up in the tree before I knew what happened. I watched him playing with his new relatives, and since he was the new kid on the block, they were teasing him as boys will do. He wound up crying, and everyone thought he was crying because his mom had gotten married. Eric and I knew better.

On to the reception, in the center of town—it was set up beautifully, and there were so many tables I was concerned about the number of guests. Well, wouldn't you know, the whole town was invited. The dining area would be open from twelve thirty to four thirty.

People were coming and going. It was the opening season for pheasant hunting, and the men would leave, shoot a few pheasants, and return to eat again. Someone decorated the car emblem with a pheasant head. This was turning out to be the most amazing wedding I had ever attended.

Next was the dance at the coliseum located in a neighboring town that happened to be about twenty miles away. "Neighboring town" meant close by to me. On the way, we saw the most beautiful sky. There were two pillars of light vertically in the horizon accented by a deep blue sky, and I saw that beautiful sky as an omen for a long and happy life together.

We arrived at the coliseum, and to my amazement, it was a large Quonset hut. Having been to the coliseum in New York City on many occasions, we were expecting something entirely different. The coliseum had been a skating rink at one time and now it was used for social events. It had a long bar on one side of the building and booths on two sides, and at the end the band was set up. It looked like some good music and fun dancing would be the order of the evening. I was right. Now two towns were invited; they all knew Dwight—he was a baseball star—and they all loved to dance. These country boys know how to drink. One of Dwight's friends fell in love with me at first sight, and I had a companion I could not shake all evening. I must admit, I was flattered. Some of the men told Tom he wasn't bad even if he did work for a large company and was from the Cities.

I did not learn for many years later, Laura had been kidnapped—a custom I presume—and she thought she would not make it to the dance. Fortunately, she did, and we were having so much fun we didn't even notice she was missing.

After the dance, our guests and Tom and I went back to our one-story motel, the only lodging in the area. We were exhausted; it was a long day and one to remember for the rest of our lives. We bless all the folks that put this wonderful wedding together. I remember Frank Sinatra singing, "I Did It My Way" and this was Rosholt, South Dakota, way. Thanks for the memory.

The years have gone by, Laura and Dwight are proud parents of Eric, Rachel, and Tori. Each child was born eight years apart, making each an only child. Their parenting skills have been remarkable. Dwight has done well in the corporate world, and Laura has been an outstanding working mom.

I often tell Laura I wish she had been my mom. I say that with all the love in my heart.

Go Figure…

A Trip to Hawaii

Winning a trip to Hawaii was exciting enough. Little did I realize how exciting it was to become.

Tom won the trip when he held the job of regional sales manager due to the many talents of his sales force. His belief that women sales representatives work harder than the men paid off.

The broken leg in a long leg cast was not going to slow me down. Tom said he would stay home if I did not want to go. Are you kidding?! I would not miss this for anything in the world.

The day before we were to leave, I was to have one bent leg cast removed, and a straight leg one would replace it. I would be able to stand on the leg. We picked up a wheelchair and decided it would travel with us. The foot rest would rise up so my leg could stretch out.

When we boarded the plane, we had a seat at the bulkhead in the front so I could prop my leg on the wall. The cast was still damp, causing my leg to feel cold. We arranged to stop in Los Angeles so we could meet our newborn grandson, Eric, and visit with our daughter Laura and her husband. The next day we were off to the airport and on to Hawaii.

The stewardesses saw me coming and the sympathy looks were for Tom. Again, we sat in the bulkhead. After we were underway, it was mai tai time, a delicious drink that Tom enjoyed. They are served with fruit stuck on a stick with a little Hawaiian baby attached to the stirrer. Tom was having fun with all the attention, and I took a pain pill.

His little babies were piling up. He was really having a good time. It was time for me to visit the ladies' room. How will I ever fit into that little bathroom with my leg sticking out straight? The stewardesses decided several of them would stand outside the door and hold a blanket up so my leg could stick out. Well, I just couldn't go with folks standing there. Finally, I jockeyed around, closed the door, and somehow hovered over the target.

When we landed, I counted eight little babies. Tom retrieved the wheelchair, sat me in it, and went to get the luggage. The company had ordered a limousine because I could not get into the bus. The limousine driver pulled up and said, "Anyone going to Kona?" A couple said, "We are." Off they went in our limousine. Now Tom showed up with the luggage, and we had no limousine.

Problem solver that he is, off he went to rent a car. They only had compact cars. He had to take the wheelchair apart to get the luggage into the trunk. Part of the wheelchair had to travel in the front seat and me in the back with the leg stretched out. By now my leg is swelling in the cast. Tom is sobering up, and I popped another pain pill.

On the way to Kona the terrain looks like the surface of the moon. We were driving along for what seemed forever, and I said, "I should not have come." I said it a few times, and Tom was saying, "Shut up, Renée." Finally, we came upon lights up ahead. We could see the hotel from a distance. We were overjoyed but do you think we could get there? We circled around and finally figured out how to get to the hotel. We pulled up in front; Tom unloaded the luggage, put the wheelchair together, and sat me in it. The man at the desk told Tom to pull the car over to the next building for check-in, but he said something meaningful to the clerk, and the clerk took the car over.

We went to our lovely room overlooking the ocean. I settled into the bed, took another pill, and slept until late the next day. Eighteen hours had gone by since arriving.

Tom pushed me around the grounds in the wheelchair. We saw the tennis courts. The trees and the plants were lovely; the ocean was clear as clear as it could be; the hotel was magnificent and the food outstanding. I was introduced to macadamia nut pie. A little bit of heaven. The people from the company were thoughtful and very nice. I was happy to be there.

The next day everyone decided to go scuba diving and insisted I go along for the ride. We went to the dock. There was a large catamaran next to the floating dock with three crew members to man it. Two of them each put a foot on the boat, kept one on the dock, and one, two, three they heaved me onto the boat in the wheelchair.

We headed out to the deep part of the ocean, and the rocking of the waves had me zooming back and forth across the deck. They anchored me down and all was well. They dropped anchor to go diving. The day was lovely and sunny, and I was enjoying the whole experience. They said if I didn't enjoy it they would use me as an anchor or maybe troll the bottom with me. What a thought.

Tom dove down and popped up by the side of the boat to tell me he saw the most remarkable fish; it was long, white, flat, and just waved around in the water in the most graceful way. The guide dove down to take a look, and it seems Tom was admiring a long strip of toilet paper.

The next morning a few men decided to play tennis, and I was to wheel over carrying the tennis rackets on my lap. A woman stopped to ask if I just fell at the courts. I found that an odd question.

Many folks would come at me with pen in hand. When I refused to let them sign the cast, they were really offended. I pictured a mess in three months and would not let them mess up my lily-white cast. They would have to get over it.

That evening we were to go to a restaurant perched on the top of a hill called the Pottery. I dressed in my muumuu, they loaded me into a limo with the wheelchair, and off we went to the restaurant. When we arrived, I looked up, and there was the longest stairway I had ever seen. The men decided they would carry me up singing, "Yo heave ho." They positioned themselves on each side of the chair and up we went.

I found it a hairy experience. I was having a lot of hairy experiences.

When inside, we were seated at a long table. The food was good; they had wonderful fresh fish and obviously very good drinks. Everyone but me was acting jolly, telling stories, laughing, drinking, and having a gay old time. It was time to leave, and these drunken men decided they would carry me down the stairs. Speaking of hair-raising, that was it! Thank God, a waiter came running over to tell them there was a ramp in the back. I was saved by a waiter. Imagine my relief.

The next night we went to a luau, and Tom asked, "Why aren't you smiling"? I had a toothache. I popped another pain pill and all was well again.

Finally, our wonderful trip was at an end. The flight home was uneventful, and by now I was comfortable with walking around in the cast.

I stopped taking the pain pills and realized I had a toothache on both sides of my mouth. My two wisdom teeth were the culprits. Tom called ahead and made an appointment with the dentist. We went from the plane to the dentist. He took one look at me in the cast and exclaimed he had never worked on someone in a cast before. We jockeyed around to get me comfortable, propping my leg on a few pillows, and he did two root canals. I was back to the pain pills.

That was some way to end a wonderful trip to Hawaii. After arriving home, I slept for eighteen hours again. I did that on both ends of the trip.

Fortunately, we had opportunities to go to Hawaii on numerous other occasions, and we loved all our adventures there.

The lesson of this story is: You can have a fun…no matter what.

Go Figure…

Sightseeing with the Kids

John was five years old, Lisa eight, Tommy nine, and Laura thirteen. At four in the morning, we loaded them into the station wagon. It had two backseats, one for each daughter, and the two boys curled up on their pillows in the back. All were sleeping within minutes, and we hoped they would sleep until we arrived in Washington, DC, for breakfast at our favorite pancake house.

After breakfast, we decided to drive around Washington so they could see the Lincoln Memorial, the Washington Monument, The Capitol Building, the cherry trees, and the White House.

We had purchased a large stack of comic books to amuse them, and they found them when we returned to the car after breakfast. As I was pointing out the sights and going on about the history of each, I looked in the backseat. They were reading comics. No one was looking out the window. Tom was driving slowly and I was yelling, "Look out the damn window!"

We decided they would like to tour the Luray Caverns. It would be a totally new experience. We checked into the motel, settled in, and no one wanted to go to the caverns. They wanted to swim in the pool. They had been swimming all summer. Once again I was yelling, "You are going to the caverns whether you want to or not, even if I have to drag you." They went and were totally unimpressed. Tom and I found it awesome. Finally we returned to the motel, and they got in the pool and were happy.

At the time there was a rock group named The Ohio Express. The girls spotted the bus at our motel and were exclaiming, "There's The Ohio Express!" Tom wanted to know how the girls knew they were from Ohio. The band members were gathered around the pool. The girls were strutting around in their cute little swim suits, diving off the board, and swimming like Ester Williams. Needless to say, the band members noticed them. They were invited to hear them practice. These were two happy girls. We didn't plan any of that, and by the way, who are The Ohio Express?

Next, we are on our way to South Carolina to spend the night at a motel called "South of the Border." They featured a zoo across the street. We figured they would enjoy the zoo, and we would go after dinner. No one wanted to go to the zoo—they wanted to swim in the pool. Again, I was yelling, "You are going to the zoo!" They went swimming after we toured the zoo and fed the elephants bags of peanuts.

Now we were headed for Grandma's sixty-acre ranch with a big house, a little house, a herd of cattle, barns, tractors, ponds, orange and grapefruit trees, cats, a pool table, and an alligator. What more could you want at a ranch? The girls were not impressed, but the boys were overjoyed. There were cousins, family members, card games, good cooking, starry nights, warm weather, and Grandma. She could call that alligator out of the pond with noises only she and the alligator understood. I forgot to mention snakes and a field of cabbage. The market was predicted to be good for cabbage that year.

The cows had calves, and the boys decided to lasso one. They did not count on an angry momma cow. They were told to get that lasso off the calf, and every time they headed toward the calf, the herd of cows headed for the boys. They were two sweaty kids, exhausted, hungry, and afraid of Grandma. She finally went out to the field before dinner and calmed down the cows. The boys removed the lasso. Tommy and John decided not to be cowboys.

The market fell flat for the cabbage. It was not worth digging out of the ground. You would not believe how large cabbage can grow. We had coleslaw, boiled cabbage, cabbage rolls, cabbage this, and cabbage that. The cows got into the cabbage patch, which is not a good thing for cows. Since they have one stomach with four digestive compartments, they can't pass gas. There they were with these huge stomachs all bloated out. It was not a good ending for the cabbage patch.

We said our good-byes to our relatives and headed for home. We stopped early at motels so that the children could swim. We made no plans for them, and they were happy.

There was one stretch of road where we found everyone friendly. People were passing us laughing, waving, giving us the thumbs up, and we were enjoying the attention. I looked in the back of the station wagon, and the two boys were holding up the centerfolds of *Penthouse* magazines on the windows. Little did I realize that Grandma had given them the magazines. Here we were tooling along, oblivious to what was going on in the back of the car.

After arriving home and settling in, we all sat down for dinner. I asked, "What did you enjoy the most on vacation?" Laura said she enjoyed when Dad bent down to tie his shoe and farted in front of the elephant.

Go Figure...

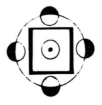

The Guests

Some guests are more welcome than others. We figured if our friends Claire and Walter stayed for a week, seven days, that would be perfect.

They were to arrive at four, and I had a wonderful dinner planned. We serve around six so that we'd avoid too long of an evening. I figured after a long evening and a lengthy drive, they would be tired and want to go to bed early. Wrong…

Around seven, we were wondering if something had happened to them. Around seven thirty they pulled into the driveway. They had started out at seven a.m. and Claire had been driving for twelve hours with the windows rolled down. Walter did not drive due to his handicap after a stroke. He believed they would save gas if they kept the windows down and the air conditioning turned off. Claire's bleach blonde hairdo and fair skin were a sight; she looked thoroughly baked and wired. Tom explained, "You do not save gas by keeping the windows down. The drag from the open windows uses more gas, not to mention the drag on the driver."

They will have to make a major investment in skin cream and hair conditioner.

Judging from the amount of luggage, it looked like they were staying for a long time, but I knew it would only be for a week. Tom and I helped them settle in, warmed up the dinner, ate, and listened to their travels until eleven thirty, when we finally excused ourselves and went to bed.

Walter loves lobster and seafood bisque; Claire is not into seafood. We found a wonderful restaurant by the lake with a lovely view, and Walter had his beloved lobster and Claire had a steak. We were pleased they were both happy and having a great time.

We decided they would like to go fishing on the lake. We had a tri-hull boat we hauled around Michigan. We hooked the boat to the car and off we went.

After dragging our fishing lines around the lake for hours, applying sunscreen, Walter got a strike on his line. He was reeling in, releasing, reeling, and releasing, just the way we suggested. He had a big one. Not far away was a small sailboat; guess what

Walter was reeling in. You guessed it. Walter was reeling and releasing the small sailboat.

A plane flew overhead, looking like a pinpoint in the sky. Claire said it was a DC-7, Walter said it was something else, and the argument was on. We listened for a while, and I suggested it was being piloted by a blue-eyed guy. A lot of their discussions went along in this vein.

It was time to take the boat out of the water. Michigan stays light until nine thirty in the summer. It was getting late, and the cars were backing up to the dock to hook up the boats. Tom and I are experienced in pulling the boat out of the water. He gets the car, backs it up to the boat while I am steadying it, I hook it up to the pulley, crank her in, and he drives up on to the road. It was obvious the man behind Tom did not know we were experienced, and when he saw Walter was handicapped, he also assumed we would take forever. He started yelling, waving his arms around, carrying on like crazy. Tom jumped out of the car, ran up to the man, and asked, "What kind of an asshole are you?" The man backed up and watched us take the boat out in five minutes flat. When I hopped in the car, I could not stop laughing, "What kind of an asshole are you?" That is the best way in the world to call someone an asshole.

The next day we decided to hang around the house so Claire's skin would get moist and her hair back to normal. Three days had gone by, only four more to go.

We did the usual sightseeing visit to downtown Detroit, dining at our favorite restaurant. We were doing well keeping them busy.

Somewhere during the visit, we were informed they were staying for two weeks. That meant nine more days. The second week Tom had to go back to work, and I was beside myself. I told Tom I was leaving, and the two teenagers were not going with me. The arguing was too much. I did not care what dog pooped on their lawn, and I don't care what kind of plane is overhead. After much thinking, we came up with a plan.

We decided Tom would be called out of town, and I had to go with him. We asked them to stay with the children until we got back.

We packed bags and went to the nearest motel. We stayed in touch with them and the kids by phone. Two days later, they informed us they were leaving for home. I explained the teens would be okay for a few days. When they pulled out of the driveway, the kids called, and we happily went home.

From then on when we are having guests, we inquire about how long they will be staying right from the beginning.

The conclusion is: visiting for a week is really okay. Visiting for two weeks is totally out of the question. I really mean out of the question.

Go Figure...

Waiting for the Christmas Painting

The Fickle Pickle restaurant is a great place to hang paintings. There is a barn behind the restaurant where a group of us get together to paint, and the only rule is you must buy lunch.

We sit out on the patio for lunch—very pleasant, good food, art conversation, a great time for sharing and talking about our creativity.

One September day while painting, a woman came into the barn asking, if a Renée Stark was present. She was interested in one of my paintings. She asked about the price and explained her son was going off to college in the fall. She was going through a divorce, was short on cash and her son loved the painting. I made an adjustment in the price, and we were both happy. She explained she would be keeping it until Christmas to surprise him.

Her son worked at the restaurant, and he had gone to the bank to get the money for the painting. When he arrived back from the bank, the painting was gone.

He asked around to see if anyone had my name and phone number. Susan, the Fickle Pickle manager, explained I was a personal friend, and she gave him my telephone number.

I received a call from a young man asking if I could paint another painting like the one I'd just sold. I put two and two together after he mentioned he was going off to college and wanted it for his dorm room. I figured he was the young son of the lady. I explained I was very busy but could probably paint another one in a month or two and asked him to give me a call when he was home for Thanksgiving.

Thanksgiving came around, and sure enough, I got a call. Now I was going to have to figure out how to stall until Christmas. He called often, and I made up excuses that were beginning to sound strange.

I toyed around with the idea of telling him his mom bought the painting because of the frequent calls. I agonized, asked friends their opinions, and all said don't even think about it. Keep making excuses.

Finally I told him I couldn't possibly have one until after Christmas.

The day after Christmas, I called him. He was delighted with the painting. I asked if he had told his mom each time he called me. He said yes, he would tell her, "I called Mrs. Stark again today, blah, blah, blah…" She must have been enjoying all of this.

The young man wanted to see my studio and any other work I might have. It would be fun to meet him. He was blond, very tall, thin, chatty, and very much at ease as we talked. He enjoyed seeing my studio, supplies, easels, paints, and paintings that were stacked up in neat rows.

He was one of the nicest young men, not at all like I pictured. He shared that he loved painting and asked interesting questions. I thank him for this wonderful adventure and the opportunity to meet a young art lover.

Thank you for giving me a Waiting for the Christmas Painting story. I hope you enjoyed your present.

Go Figure…

Hindenburg

This story is a childhood memory that takes place May 6, 1937.

Our family lived in Browns Mills, New Jersey. It was a small town. We lived in Browns Mills because it was close to Camp Dix. Dad was in the military stationed at Camp Dix, then a tent community; now it's called Fort Dix. I remember the military men at that time wore jodhpurs, boots, what they called a Sam Brown belt, which went around the waist and had a belt that went over the shoulder. They wore a hat with a bill. Looking back on the outfit, it wasn't practical, but I thought my dad was very handsome in his uniform.

While living in a cabin-type house located under the pines, we had a German shepherd, Peggy. When I was younger, we had Scotties. President Roosevelt had a Scottie named Falla, and they became the dog of the day. Everyone wanted a Scottie. They are wonderful little dogs.

I learned to swim in a lake located across the street. Under our house was a crawl space that housed a canoe. Dad cleaned it up, and I became proficient at canoeing. Since I was a good swimmer, I was allowed to go canoeing by myself, and that was the beginning of my love affair with boating. Dad and I would go out in the boat to pick blueberries along the shore. Those are precious memories.

While we lived there, I contracted measles, and at that time, you had to stay in a darkened room for seven days to avoid blindness. It was a long week. Fortunately, today we know that blindness and being in a dark room is not true.

My sister ran away from home at the age of five. She moved in with the neighbors next door and refused to come home. Every time they tried to bring her home, she would scream and kick, frustrating Mom and Dad. They finally figured out the neighbors were letting her do anything she wanted and stay up late. I don't know how it was resolved, but she did come home to live once again. She always had a mind of her own.

In the small school, I tried out for a singing contest. This would be my big day, and I was ready. I knew all the words, my hair was in curls, and I was dressed like Shirley Temple. Surely I would win. I came in second.

It was crushing not to be the winner. No one told me I could not sing. I could throw my hat in the air higher than anyone else could.

One day, the *Hindenburg* flew over our house and it was a sight I will always remember. It was flying low, getting ready to land, giving us a closeup view of this huge ship.

I was eight years old at the time, and my sister was five.

The *Hindenburg* burned upon landing at the airstrip near the town of Lakehurst, New Jersey. The *Hindenburg* was a Nazi German dirigible, and this was the maiden voyage. All eyes were on this event since it was the first flight of this kind.

The balloon was filled with hydrogen to keep it airborne. The travelers were below the balloon in a large cabin where everyone on board resided. The accommodations were very comfortable.

Dad wanted to see the *Hindenburg* land, and we were off to Lakehurst in our car. When we got close to the landing site, traffic was moving slowly. As we neared the airfield, we could see flames and smell smoke. People were rushing around and strange hissing noises from the fire filled the air. My sister and I did not know what was going on until years later.

We knew our mother was frightened and insisted we leave. Reluctantly, Dad turned the car around to head for home. We were in the backseat, and our parents told us not to look out the window. Being curious, we looked and we put our heads down on the backseat. We headed for home, and Dad was listening to the events on the radio.

The announcer was saying, "Oh my God! People are dying…jumping out of the fiery cabin to their deaths." Flames were everywhere, and some people made it out of the cabin alive. The announcer was hysterical while reporting what he was seeing. Men were holding the anchor lines while the smoke billowed around them. Thirty-six people died in the fiery crash. The announcer was at the site and gave a minute-by-minute report as things were happening on the ground. The broadcast was extremely frantic, but it was an accurate account of what was happening.

Go Figure…

Waiting for the Plane

The airport provides you with all kinds of entertainment. Here is where my story begins.

I looked around, trying to find a quiet place to sit while waiting for a plane. The seats near the gate were filled, so I chose a seat across the way so I could see my gate clearly.

Settling in for some good, old people-watching along came a young man, very blond, quite handsome, short, casually dressed, big blue eyes, very tanned, and I smiled. Before I knew it, he'd settled into the seat next to me. We exchanged pleasantries, and the following conversation began.

"Why are you in Florida?"

I explained my sister was ill, and she spent time in the hospital. I'd been with her for two weeks, and it was time to go home. "Why are you in Florida?"

He explained, "There is a group of people on the Internet that volunteer to go to Florida to thin out alligators in the Everglades. Only a certain number are accepted in the country, and people wait on lists for a long time. I was fortunate to have been chosen. Once in Florida, we're trained in capturing the alligator, getting it into the boat, and the trainers do the rest."

I did not want to know what "do the rest" meant. The alligator hunt in the Everglades was interesting. Males can be eleven feet long, sometimes weighing a thousand pounds; females grow to be eight feet long, and they can live to be fifty to sixty years old. The Everglade Alligator Farm has over two thousand alligators, and they are all sizes. The hunt is a limited time each summer. The waiting list for volunteers is long due to interested people. I had no idea this took place in the Everglades.

He went on to explain he was a recovering alcoholic, he was active in AA, and his church had provided the money for his trip. He had been a womanizer for years and was ashamed of the fact.

Now he had a wonderful girlfriend. His phone rang, he took the call, and when he finished, he explained the call was from his wonderful girlfriend.

She lived in Puerto Rico. I asked if he was planning to marry her. He said she wanted to marry him, but he was not ready for a commitment. He had many issues to resolve.

His flight was announced; it was time to board the plane. We hugged each other, wished each other well, and off he went.

I was provided with all kinds of entertainment while waiting for my plane. The airport is an amazing place. Who would have thought I would have an education on how to thin out alligators in the Everglades? Especially from a young recovering alcoholic who was turning his life around.

I am grateful for having had this conversation with this darling young man. Let us hope all is well with him. I doubt he will remember. Remembering our brief meeting somehow makes me feel good, and now I know more about alligators.

A smile and listening skills allows all kinds of interesting connections with people. They usually are not interested in what you have to say; they just want someone to listen.

For some strange reason, I think of that young man often and picture him married, with a couple of kids, active in church, and living in a cottage with a white picket fence.

Go Figure...

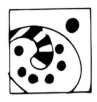

Life Is Buggy

Mary and Paul sent us the most beautiful floral centerpiece one year for Christmas. It arrived in the longest box, and I knew I didn't have a vase long enough for those roses. When I opened the box there was a tall vase and pine greens and fifteen white tiger lilies. They fit into our color scheme: red doesn't fit in an orange environment. Mary gave this gift a lot of thought. When the lilies opened, they were as big as saucers. Each day they brought a new visual delight.

When it was time to take the lilies out, I kept the greens in the vase in the kitchen.

One day, I noticed a small bug walking around the counter. I decided to look at her with a magnifying glass; she was lovely. She was almond shaped: her head attached to the round part of the almond, her body looked like a bronze tortoise shell edged with white dots. The point part of the almond looked like a pinecone, and I felt she hatched from the pine greens. Her antennas were long and black. She had three legs on each side. Each leg had two knees allowing her to walk sideways, forward, and backward. I was having fun watching her walking around, and I kept putting her on the pines. I named this creature Sara.

Sara disappeared, and Tom and I kept an eye out for her. Tom noticed her walking around on the glass table in the living room. We wondered how she'd arrived there, maybe walking down the wall, across the carpet, and up the table. I put her back on the greens.

On Saturday night, we play cards with a couple, and we told them about Sara's journey. They suggested she could fly. At that point, we forgot all about Sara since she was no longer in the greens.

A week later we were watching TV and our cat, Pearl, was looking at the lamp next to me. She had spotted Sara, and then Sara flew to the wall. She was on her way to hide behind a painting. I scooped her up, and since she could fly, I dropped her off our balcony five stories up. I pray Sara had a gentle landing.

The next night Pearl was looking at the wall again; there was the same kind of bug, and this time he was bigger. I scooped him up and dropped him off the balcony to join his wife Sara.

Go Figure

The following night, out comes a baby from behind the painting. Out it went, off the balcony. Enough already! Time has gone by and no more beautiful bugs.

We live in an apartment at The Summit, and we were to have a bed bug inspection. When the day came, we were home, and we had a chance to meet the dog, Sunny, the bed bug sniffer. He was cute as a bug, medium sized, black, white, and tan beagle. Sunny is with his handler twenty-four hours a day.

His handler explained they travel from facility to facility up and down the east coast, across the southern part of the United States, and up the state of California.

I asked how his wife adjusted to his schedule, and he explained his wife died some years ago. He could have been in his mid-forties. Later I found out he owns a sailboat on Lake Lanier where he and Sunny live when they are in Georgia.

Our cats, George and Pearl, were hiding from Sunny. George hid in the closet, and Pearl hid under the bed. We watched Sunny do his sniffing, and they were on their way to the next apartment.

It is amazing what dogs can do. Seeing the handler and Sunny working together was a joy. The devotion of man and his dog is wonderful to see.

People do not have that kind of relationship with bugs. I became attached to Sara and respected her beauty, truly one of Earth's mysterious creations.

One morning I went out to breakfast, which I seldom do. There was a man wearing a T-shirt that was printed on the front. It read "Roaches Pub," complete with a crest from Ireland. I had no idea roaches had pubs.

I wish I had a T-shirt that read, "My Bug Sara." I have painted her portrait so I will always remember beautiful Sara. I pray the family is living happily five stories down.

Go Figure…

The Presidents

I had recently finished commercial art school at Oakland Community in Farmington Hills. My son and daughter were in high school at that time, and we were all busy doing homework.

After school, I found I needed people energy to be creative, and I had become isolated while going to school with my best friend Jean. She moved away, and I needed to do something other than art.

United Way was looking for volunteers, and I wound up interviewing people to fill other volunteer needs. I answered one of the requests for an interviewer at the 48th District Court. It sounded interesting and challenging. The office was in the Court House in Birmingham, Michigan. It was an easy drive from my home.

I interviewed offenders and made recommendations for sentencing. This part of the probation office was to help judges make decisions to ease their workload. After a few months, I realized they needed a training manual for the volunteers. There were strict guidelines, rules, and regulations. We interviewed from a list of questions and from there we would gather all the information about the crime that was committed.

It was important to be objective, have accurate listening skills, a nonjudgmental attitude, and above all, no personal involvement. I put together the training manual for the volunteers.

The cases were interesting. One lady had stolen a teddy bear from a store. I asked what was going on in her life, and she said she had cancer, her husband had just left her, her parents moved away, and when she saw the teddy bear she took it. You don't throw the book at someone with this kind of story.

Another time, I was asked to interview a young man about seventeen years old. Everyone in the office seemed to be anxious about this interview. The young man arrived in torn shorts, sandals, sleeveless tee shirt, messy hair, and stubble on his face. Not exactly the dress of the day for the probation department. We went into the interview room, and he proceeded to tell me he was arrested for beating his car up while drunk. He hung it up on a hill of dirt so that the wheels were not touching the ground, he got out and bashed all the windows out and beat all the fenders.

We spent a long time talking; he told me about himself, answered all the questions from the questionnaire, and we had a great discussion. When we came out of the interview room, we gave each other a hug, and he left. My supervisor asked how the interview went. I said great. She told me he was interviewed at another probation department, and he'd attacked the interviewer. He had anger management issues. No wonder they were all concerned. I was not concerned.

A DUI brought a man around forty to the probation department. He admitted he was drinking and should not have been driving. I asked, "What were you doing that alerted the officer?" He said he was going slowly and being very careful. I asked, "Where were you when you were driving slowly?"

He replied, "I was driving on the median."

A young truck driver came in for a stealing crime. When asked where the police found the things he had stolen, he said he had hidden them in his truck. He had added the police didn't find the things he had stolen the day before. I suggested we just stick to the crime for which he was arrested.

Sometime in the late seventies, Presidents Nixon, Carter, Johnson, and Ford visited Birmingham, Michigan. I'm not sure of the exact date. They gave short comments on the lawn at the court house on the square in Birmingham, Michigan. The crowd was thrilled to see four presidents visit their fair city on the back lawn on a beautiful fall day. We were seeing four presidents gathered together. They said a few patriotic words and then stood around for pictures, making it a great photo opportunity. It was an exciting event.

Even more exciting, Donny Osmond sang "The Star-Spangled Banner." Donny Osmond, everyone loved Donny Osmond. My daughter was in love with Donny Osmond. Later, I found out Donny Osmond sat at my desk in the probation office before he was to sing. He chatted with the staff and gave each one a big hug before he left. They said he was very nice, friendly, and handsome.

I ask you, would you rather be hugged by Donny Osmond or listen to the presidents? I just don't know.

Go Figure...

Valerie Was My Sister

I was asked to speak first at my sister's funeral, and I felt I was up to the task. I traveled from Atlanta to Denver, and Kellie, my niece, picked me up at the airport. Kellie is my sister's oldest of three children.

I remember the day Valerie was born in the front room of our house; I was four years old. I had a baby sister who was always smiling and she was a cute little baby, my live baby doll.

When she was four, Daddy married a new mom, and the new mom had a daughter Nanette. Valerie had a playmate in Nanette who was five. They became best friends immediately.

Our brother Lucky, sometimes called John, was born, and we all became babysitters. He kept us busy, we spoiled him rotten. We took turns pushing him in a carriage around and around outside the house so he would sleep. We did everything for him, gave him his first ice cream cone—a memorable experience—changed his diapers, and carried him around like a play toy.

Vicki was born in New Jersey when we lived in Penns Grove, New Jersey. We all went to the hospital to pick her up. We went to the nursery and looked through the window at the babies. We picked out a chunky dark-haired darling, and Mom said, "That is not our baby. It's this one," pointing to a scrawny little bald baby. We all came to love her cute little self. Valerie now shared her life with one brother and three sisters.

I called our sister Nanette in Florida because she couldn't join us for the funeral due to health issues. I asked her if she wanted to say something at the memorial service. She replied, "Some people call a blended family a broken home, and our home was never broken. If I could have picked a sister, I would pick her again in a minute."

I remember the crazy things those girls did. They dressed alike, and Mom bought them new shoes with ration points during WWII. These ration points allowed you to buy two pairs of shoes a year. There they were outside on the sidewalk rubbing the shoes on the pavement. When asked what they were doing, they said they didn't like the shoes—they wanted boots. Mom bought them boots and prayed their feet didn't grow. They would get all dressed up in dresses and their black boots. They were as happy as larks. Both girls were always together, living in their little girl world.

There was a time we all shared a bedroom, three single beds in a row; each bed had a pastel color, pink, blue, and mint green. We each had a vanity with ruffles the picture of femininity. We loved our beautiful bedroom, and Mom made all the spreads and ruffles.

The three of us would babysit when there were activities on the army post. People would drop their children off at our house, and we three would keep track of them for 25 cents an hour.

When growing up, the three of us, Billy, and the kids across the street would play dodge ball until the streetlights went on. We knew we had to go inside to bed. Back then, we all went to bed early. We three would talk and giggle for hours with Mom yelling, "Quiet down up there."

Little did we realize later in life Valerie and Bill would make a lifetime commitment.

We both rented our first apartment in the same complex, and we ate together often. Looking back, our apartments were small but all our own. We spent many vacations together with trips to the New Jersey Shore and to Florida with all our little kids packed into the backseat. We had many fun adventures.

In our later years, we got together for sister time every March. We would get together for five days to eat, play games, cards, and Scrabble. Mostly we laughed. When we were together, there was always laughter. Not just a little chuckle, but tears rolling down our faces laughter.

Valerie's biggest joys were her children, grandchildren, and great-grandchildren. She spoke of them often. A grandmother has no greater love than for her family.

I am grateful for having Valerie for a sister, for the lessons her life taught me, her faith, friendship, laughter, and most of all her children. She dearly loved each and every one of them.

She made me an Aunt Renée and there is nothing more rewarding than that.

I will miss her, and I am grateful for the peace she is experiencing right now. She will always be in our hearts.

Go Figure…

The Dancing Lady

This story begins in the summer of 1939 when Tom was ten years old. Tom was a lean little kid with dark brown eyes, dark brown curly hair, tan as a water chestnut with a mischievous way about him.

He spent the summer working for a vegetable man, running from the truck to the customer, delivering the fruit and vegetables and collecting the money. He was paid a small sum for his services, and he was having a wonderful summer.

His Aunt Tillie worked in a curio shop downtown, and he would walk to the store to visit his beloved aunt and look around the store. He wanted to buy his mother a present with the money he was saving but had not decided how much he could spend or what the gift should be.

Finally, on one visit to the store, he spotted the most beautiful Dancing Lady figurine. It was a graceful woman dancing with an outstretched arm holding her black skirt out to the side, head thrown slightly back, delicate features, and strapless top. Knowing how long it took him to save the money, his mom was delighted with the first gift her youngest son had ever given her. She placed it on top of the TV in the front room for all to see. When Tom's mom passed away, we were given the Dancing Lady, and I kept it in our China closet for years. When it came time for us to sell our house and move to The Summit, an independent living facility, Tom gave the Dancing Lady to our oldest daughter, Laura.

Tom had given our son his drum set some years ago and like his dad, he has become a talented drummer. He plays my favorite jazz. He decided to refurbish the drums and design a logo.

Our son, Thomas Kevin, called asking about the Dancing Lady figurine; if we had it, and if not, where was it. He recalled seeing it on Grandma's TV when he was a little boy and wanted to put it on the drum set. We explained Laura had it. She sent him a picture of it on the computer so he could reproduce it for the drum.

During this time, Thomas Kevin was diagnosed with Hodgkin's lymphoma. Our boy was ready for the fight of his life. He researched everything anyone could have possibly known about this cancer. He had cells in his bone marrow, lymph nodes, and was diagnosed at stage four.

Fortunately, he had heard of Dr. Kiminski and his treatment with Bexxar. After much testing, Thomas was accepted into the program at the University of Michigan in Ann Arbor. After forty-two difficult days, Thomas was cancer-free! His work was finished, and we all breathed a sigh of relief. Chances of a recurrence after ten years are slim, and we are grateful.

Now the year is 2012. Thomas and his wife planned a fundraiser for cancer treatment. They arranged a dinner with a wonderful meal, music, and dancing. Thomas was playing with the band and there was the Dancing Lady on his drum for all to see.

Go Figure…

The Orientals Next Door

We lived on a sloping hill, and the house next to us was slightly raised from our property. Sitting by the kitchen windows, we had a lovely view of the Orientals' back yard. A beautiful crabapple tree stood in front of our window, and in the spring it was a sight to behold, blooms everywhere.

The Orientals next door owned a clothes-cleaning establishment. They were very private. The first time I spoke to the little woman was when she was digging up some of the plants on our property to plant in her yard.

In the spring, she and her husband planted a garden where we could watch things grow from our kitchen window. They buried fish under the plants, and the dog who lived on the other side of our house would dig up the plants. It was fun to watch.

One day after another planting, we looked out and there were lampshades all over the garden acting as little greenhouses. When the lampshades were removed, we viewed a corn crop. Amazing. Farming was not allowed in our subdivision.

We had a heavy rain, and they had parked a truck on the hill behind their house that we viewed from our kitchen table—not exactly scenic. They went to move the truck while we were having lunch. The truck would not back up because of the wet grass. We'd had a heavy rain the night before. He was spinning the wheels, creating masses of grass flying, and then large hunks of mud flew out the back. What a sight; we were laughing so hard we were crying.

Wonderfully creative, out comes the little woman with some throw rugs. They put them under the wheels and out flew throw rugs each time they spun the wheels. They were truly named Throw Rugs. Out came another stack of rugs, and by now we are roaring with laughter. Each time a new rug flew, we would lose it laughing.

They finally drove the truck out of the yard, and it was never parked there again.

We planted Leland cedars all along that side of the property, staggering them for a good shield, making a good barrier. We placed them eight feet away from our property line.

Well, wouldn't you know they planted trees right up against our cedars on our property. We figured, the hell with it, we will just prune their trees if they get intrusive, which we did often. I understand the new owner of our house sued them for planting trees on her property.

The laughter we enjoyed that day was a gift to remember them by.

Bless them and keep them and hope I will never see them again.

Go Figure...

Europe, Here We Come

The *Queen Mary* was docked at the New York Pier in all her splendor. The air was filled with excitement as travelers and guests boarded for pre-sailing festivities.

We arranged a party for family and friends to see us off to London for a three-month stay, and then we were to move on to Göteborg, Sweden. We planned to stay in Sweden for two years then move on to Germany.

A bell sounded, and all guests were escorted from the ship. Most of the travelers went out on the decks. They were waving farewell to the guests and the New York Harbor. In January, the air and wind were chilling, the sea was calm, and New York City shimmered in the sunlight. We stayed on deck until the city disappeared from view.

Two staterooms were to be home for six days. The children, John only one at the time and Lisa, age four, were assigned a space in the nursery. Their time on board would be spent supervised and playing with the other children on board until evening.

I was young, lean, animated, easy to smile, and full of adventure. My new life was unfolding. My first husband, Lee, was bright, lean, and lanky at six foot two inches tall; he was personable, extremely bright, impeccably dressed, never looked harried, and always quick to laugh. He made friends easily.

Lee was working for a large oil company for their research and engineering. He had an assignment with the largest steel manufacturers in England. When that project was complete, he would move on to Sweden. There was an oil refinery in Göteborg where they planned to build underground storage in rock formations for oil. Ships came in and out of the port for refueling.

The plan was to live in an apartment on Bryanston Square in London, England. We were neighbors to the Swedish Embassy. Living in London was a totally new experience for us both. The apartment had a kitchen, dining room, bedroom, and bath on the lower level. Street level was a bedroom complete with mirrored furniture, living room, and foyer. The windows were floor to ceiling, looking out on the courtyard garden. Heavy drapes hung on the windows, left from blackout days during WWII. They were always open during the day.

The living room had Victorian furniture and an ornate clock, complete with cherubs, golden scrolls, and heavy gold candlesticks on the mantle. The fireplace was black marble and was an exact duplicate of the fireplace at Number 10 Downing Street. There were inlaid parquet floors throughout in a beautiful herringbone pattern.

The children, John and Lisa slept in the bedroom located on the first floor and our au pair, Ingrid, slept in an alcove in the dining room near the children. She was from Oslo, Norway, and was learning English from me, so she spoke English with an American accent.

Refrigeration was a small box that only held a day's worth of food. Milk was delivered in bottles—with rich cream on the top—each Monday, Wednesday, and Friday. Shopping was done each day for the evening meal.

Four o'clock tea was a delightful hour of the day, and I think the world would be a better place if everyone observed this tradition. Small sandwiches, scones, and biscuits were served as well. Most families fed their children around six, and the adults ate at eight or nine after the children were settled in bed.

Ingrid and I walked everywhere in London. We had a double stroller or "pram" as the Brits called it. We would settle the children in it and off we would go. Our favorite walk was to the London Zoo. The animals and gardens were spectacular.

Lisa went to nursery school on Baker Street. We would walk to Baker Street, and she would hop and skip along looking forward to having playmates. On our way, we would walk through narrow streets and pass small shops. Each sold a different item, meat in one, in others vegetables, fruit, and pastries. We enjoyed the aromas and visual delights of fresh foods.

We had a wedding for Ingrid. She married a Norwegian sea captain, named Arild. She had a lovely wedding aboard the Norwegian freighter that Arild piloted. She wore one of my white evening gowns for the wedding and looked lovely.

John, not yet a year old, spent time with her, and she had been speaking Norwegian to him. We had studied Swedish before our trip, and we were speaking English.

While in London, we flew to Paris with Lisa to buy a red sports car, leaving John with Ingrid, and we visited the plant where the cars were manufactured. We drove it to Calais where the car was loaded onto a plane for the trip back to London. The car was kept in a garage not far from our apartment. I didn't have a European license; therefore, I would not be driving in England. Weekends were for sightseeing and driving the car around London.

The day came when it was time to move to Sweden just as spring arrived in London. I did not want to go. I said, "I feel our life will be over." Lee laughed, saying, "Don't be silly; our life has been planned."

Ingrid was to take the train from London to Gravesend where we would board the ship to Göteborg. The red sports car had a roof that could be removed, weather permitting. On our journey, we were running late, and Lee was speeding down winding roads, past green meadows, fields of grazing sheep everywhere.

Ingrid, John, and Lisa had arrived at the ship, and we checked the car in for loading. We had two cabins, one for Ingrid and the children, and one for us. The ship's cabins were compact, and we were sleeping in bunks.

The trip would take the afternoon and evening, arriving after breakfast. In the evening we sat in the lounge and watched the children play then went to our cabins.

Lee was reading *A View from the Terrace*, and I climbed into the lower bunk and promptly went to sleep. We all met for breakfast. John was restless, and we played peek-a-boo with a napkin. All of us were filled with anticipation, not knowing what the day would bring. We knew we would have a full day in our new experience.

Someone from the company was to meet us, take us to the hotel, and in the afternoon, they were to have a reception so I could meet the wives and their husbands associated with the company.

Our driver was at the dock to take us to the hotel while Lee waited for the car to be unloaded. I remember leaving the dock with the children and Ingrid and waving good-bye as he stood on the dock. Off we went.

We checked into our room, settled our bags in, and waited until Lee joined us. The day was lovely, sunny, and warm. One hour, two hours, three hours passed, and I decided everyone should take a bath and change clothes to ease the waiting. We all bathed and dressed. I decided we should go to the dining room for lunch. I was worried by this time, and I wondered if Lee had gone to the refinery. I showed off my Swedish by ordering in Swedish. The waiters and waitresses were extremely attentive, looking over our way and whispering. I thought, *They don't see well-behaved American children often.* We finished our meals, and there was nothing else to do but go back to the room.

I opened the door to the room and stepped inside to find three couples in our room. What a strange reception. The children and Ingrid were quickly ushered down the hall on some pretense.

Someone said, "There has been an accident."

Worried, I replied, "What hospital is he in? He's strong and will recover quickly."

They just looked at me and said, "He's gone."

From somewhere outside of myself I heard screams.

The director of the refinery took us to his home to stay until the shock had worn off and we could make plans to return to the United States. Needless to say, the tears would not stop. My heart was completely broken. I was given a sedative and went to sleep. My children were in good hands. They were playing with the director's daughter who was Lisa's age. His wife read them stories after they settled in to bed.

Lee's company sent for my mother and Lee's uncle to help me return to the United States and made all the arrangements for the family members to fly home. On my mother's second evening there, Lisa awoke screaming "Daddy! Daddy!" and I believe he came to her and was saying good-bye. Her grandmother sat with her until she settled down and fell into a fitful sleep.

We boarded a plane for Gatwick, Ireland, and from there we changed planes for JFK in NYC. While at Gatwick, we toured the airport and let the children run and play. We had a long flight ahead of us. On the bulkhead the stewardess attached a crib for one-year-old John and Lisa slept between her grandmother and Uncle Jim.

The funeral was three weeks after Lee's death. His body was processed through JFK airport to a funeral home in Bergenfield, New Jersey. Our life together was over, and it was hard to believe.

The adoption agency that handled John's adoption called about two weeks after arriving in the US to say they had reviewed my test scores and decided I was strong enough and financially secure enough to raise him. They would let me keep him. The terms of the adoption clearly stated that if a member were to die before the adoption was finalized, the child would go back to the agency. We'd planned ahead because we were going out of the country, so Lee and I had signed all of the papers ahead of time.

I later found out that Lee was killed on a bridge entering Göteborg. Traffic stopped when the crash occurred; he got out of the car and collapsed. Some folks picked him up and put him in a small sports car to take him to the hospital. A broken rib punctured his lung and caused his death. I feel if they had not moved him, he would not have died. He was 6'2", not the size you could lay down in a small car. Unfortunately, I did not see Lee after he died. To this day, I sometimes dream that he is living in Sweden.

His death caught international attention in the papers and the news. Stories and pictures of the accident were in the Swedish and New York newspapers.

I had furniture scattered all over the globe: in the home we owned in Morris Plains, New Jersey, in England, and some in an apartment in Göteborg, Sweden. The car was a total loss.

The house we owned in Morris Plains, New Jersey, was sold, and the children and I settled into

Grandma's for a few months. We then moved into a small house on a quiet street in the town of Bergenfield, New Jersey.

This was to be the end of one story, but the beginning of another amazing one.

Go Figure…

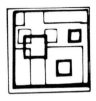

Dinner with Whom?

Cooking dinner for the Japanese was out of the question. They shot at my father in World War II. My dad was in the Pacific for two years, and I really missed him. I was not having them to our home for dinner.

Tom asked, "Would you join us for dinner at a restaurant?" I agreed. Neutral ground. He'd made plans to take them to our favorite dining spot and requested his special very blonde waitress. When we arrived, the guests from the Japanese international company were waiting for us. Introductions were made, we were seated, and the thought occurred to me these folks were really nice. They had been working with Tom for some time, and it was obvious that they held him in great esteem. Tom was an expert at negotiating with the Japanese.

As the evening progressed, I was having a wonderful time with these little men dressed in black suits and white shirts. There was laughter, great stories, good food, excellent service, and drinking. They became enamored with our lovely blonde waitress. The president of the company wanted her to become Burger Queen of Japan, to give you an idea of the drinking part. Before the evening ended, I suggested to Tom that we should have them to the house for a cook out. He was delighted.

The next day, I planned the menu, knowing that steak, melons, tomatoes, and corn on the cob were priceless in Japan. My butcher had provided us with the loveliest steaks; I bought tomatoes, melons, and corn from a nearby farm. It being summer, these fruits and vegetables would be at their best. This menu would be a treat for our Japanese friends, and I could not have planned a better meal for them. We had a coworker from the company wear an apron, serve drinks, and cook the steaks on the grill.

They had never been to an American home and were excited about the invitation. I also invited a young couple from the neighborhood with their five-year-old son so they could experience a typical American couple.

The house was sparkling clean. We had a patio ringed with evergreens looking out over a park—a lovely setting. The table was set in the dining room, platters were out, and the bar was set up. The stage was set.

They arrived on time, and all was very formal—much bowing and smiling. After the second drink, everyone seemed to relax. All of a sudden, I noticed they were walking toe-to-heel the length of the family room. They were measuring how many tatami mats wide the room was. They paced off the living room, kitchen, foyer, and study. It seemed they were everywhere. Next, they asked if they could see what was in the kitchen cabinets, especially the spices I had been using.

They seemed to be enjoying the young couple and their child, asking all kinds of questions about their lives. Our guests experienced a well-behaved, bright, blond child, and they enjoyed talking with him. In Japan, there are no blond children.

It was time to eat, the grill was going, the steaks were piling up, platters of tomatoes, melons, and huge platters of corn were on the patio tables. Our guests came out to the patio with their cameras and our chef started posing. They pushed him away from the grill because they wanted to photograph the platter of steaks. It was fun just watching them have fun.

After the joyous meal, we gathered around in the family room, and we had a chance to talk about the news of the day. In Japan, the women do not gather with the men or go to business dinners. Having the hostess and the young couple participate in the discussion was new to them. The accident at the Three Mile Island nuclear facilities had just happened, and it was a major concern. The discussion about safety and nuclear plants was interesting.

After the discussion and tea, we moved into the living room where Tom provided some entertainment. I forgot to mention, everyone had drinks with dinner and after-dinner drinks. Tom did a pantomime to an old record of "The Sow Song" about a pig—complete with pig sound effects—and then pantomimed a hilarious cowboy song with sound effects. The laughter was filling up the house. What a joyous evening! Everyone had a great time, most of all me.

This evening was the beginning of a long and productive relationship between the two companies involved. They went on to invite us on a trip to Japan. That is another story.

To think I did not want to meet these Japanese businessmen boggles my mind.

Go Figure…

The Spiritualist

Going to a spiritualist was a new experience and I had no idea what to expect.

I rang the doorbell. A tall, lanky intense woman opened the door and led me into a small sitting room. I sat down and made myself comfortable in the cozy room. She explained I could ask five questions, and she would answer them. There was a charge for the visit, and I paid her before we began.

She put a tape into her radio and explained she would tape the session so that I could refer to it later.

Two of the questions I remember. I asked, "Why am I never concerned about money," and "How is it that I can read palms?" I truly know nothing about palm reading, but I can accurately come up with the past and future. I seem to know more about the future.

She explained that I was a Gypsy in a previous life. I had my hand out for money all the time, and I wore large rings. In this life, we have had all the money we needed, no matter what the circumstances.

She said my husband was a Greek ship captain. I found that interesting. When I was a child, I used to pretend my father was Greek. He had dark hair and very dark brown eyes, but he was French and English. Tom has brown eyes, a dark complexion, and dark hair, and maybe he could have been a Greek ship captain. He is actually Irish, but a black Irishman, as they say.

I have always worn very large rings in this life. When I look into someone's palm while holding their hand, I pick up information without even thinking about it. Sometimes I think it is intuition and some kind of cosmic energy.

When I married Tom, we bought a Chris Craft 36-foot boat that slept six. It was a wonderful ship, powered by two diesel engines. Tom didn't know anything about the sea, and when he took the helm, it was as though he had been piloting all his life. Could he have been the sea captain in a previous life? The spiritualist awakened true stories that were uncovered during my life adventures.

The spiritualist said, "The sea captain wanted children, and you did not."

Tom had his two children from a previous marriage, and I wanted children but couldn't have them. I adopted a girl and a boy. When we married, all of a sudden I had four children. Another fortuneteller at the New Jersey Shore told me, when I was thirty-three, I would have four children, and I said, "That is impossible." She was right. I have four children. Oddly enough, my two daughters, just by chance, are named Lisa Lyn and Laura Lynn. The boys are Thomas John and Thomas Kevin. Both girls are born Aquarius and both boys Aries. Tom and I were born eight hours apart, and we are Leos. It made an interesting family.

In talking to my mother after visiting the spiritualist, it seems we had Gypsies in our family tree. She never mentioned it for fear I would be ashamed. The Gypsies were from Greece and migrated to Spain, and my distant grandmother fled Spain during the Franco-Prussian War.

My mother's mother was born in Copenhagen, Denmark, and her grandmother was born in Spain. My great-grandmother was with a circus and performed as a high-wire act with her husband. In Copenhagen, both fell from the high wire and were killed. They had a little girl, my grandmother, who was eight years old when they died. Her daughter moved to the US with her German husband, had a nervous breakdown when my mother was eight. She lived the rest of her days in a mental institution in New York State. The age of eight seems to be bad luck in my family. My mother ran off with a man when I was eight years old, leaving me behind. There seems to be a pattern here.

While traveling in Greece, we saw Gypsy communities and both of us had strange feelings seeing them. It all seemed familiar. How did the spiritualist know? She told me all about the past, and I seem to know about the future.

What does all this mean? Who knows?

Go Figure…

Go to Alaska, Okay?

The phone call came from my much younger sister, Vicki. She said Mom was sick and had been taken off a plane to the Philippines in Anchorage, Alaska. Aunt Maude was traveling with Mom. She reported the doctors at the hospital said Mom would not make it.

Mom and Aunt Maude had been on the way to Philippine faith healers to remove the cancer from Mom's body. They had removed her cataracts on a previous trip, to the amazement of her eye doctor, and she was sure they could do something for her to make her well. Aunt Maude was convinced also. I really don't know where I stand on this whole idea of Philippine faith healers.

Years ago when Mom was fifteen, Aunt Maude had been taking their mother to the grocery store, and as she was crossing the train tracks, the train crashed into the car, killing their mother. Six children suddenly were motherless. From then on Aunt Maude was on call for all the members of the family when needed. It was her way of coping and paying back. She was a great caregiver, and when you started to get well, she would get upset because you no longer needed her. Aunt Maude was determined to support my mother in whatever way she could, including going to the Philippines with her.

When you fly to the Philippines, you go over the top of our planet, stopping in Anchorage for refueling. Mom's brother and sister-in-law, Henry and Nora, have lived in Anchorage for years.

All of her children—Valerie, Nanette, Lucky, my brother, Vicki, and I—were all flying to Alaska from our various locations. Valerie from Denver, Nanette from Ft. Myers, Vicki from Dallas, Lucky from Dothan, Alabama, and at the time, I was living near Detroit. We siblings were scattered all over the place.

The day before the flight, Nanette broke her toe on a bookcase at home making traveling difficult. She arrived on crutches. Nanette hobbled around for the duration of the visit and would sit down at every opportunity.

Tom booked a flight to Alaska for me. The flight I was to take would have a layover in Chicago. The day before, that same numbered flight had crashed in Chicago, killing everyone on board. The plane I was on was nearly empty due to the crash. It was the most pleasant flight I had ever taken. Not one screaming kid, perfect service, and plenty of room to stretch out.

Uncle Henry met me at the airport. For some reason I will never understand, I took a large suitcase that weighed a ton. Uncle Henry was annoyed with me from the beginning. Usually he was annoyed with me after a couple of hours. Because I'd taken a big suitcase, he must have thought I was planning to stay for months. I was determined to look lovely while in Alaska to visit Mom. Not knowing how long our stay would be, I was prepared for everything—hot weather, cold weather, you name it.

My siblings had already arrived and had nestled in. I was to room with Valerie, my full sister; my stepsister Nanette and my half-sister Vicki were rooming together. My half-brother Lucky was sleeping on the living room couch.

Aunt Nora announced she was cooking a turkey, and we were delighted. We would have a turkey dinner and then go to the hospital to see Mom. Aunt Nora was flakey, but interesting. She had put the bird in the pressure cooker, and it was a mess. This was to be our turkey dinner? We all piled in the car and went out for a seafood dinner before we went to the hospital.

Mom and Aunt Maude were in good spirits, and Mom was feeling comfortable. We were assured she was in good hands, and we were relieved when we knew she was in a fine hospital with two caring doctors. Her care could not have been better.

In June in Alaska, the sun goes down for a few minutes, and the five of us visited all night, laughing at the crazy things we would do as children. We were all raised differently: Vicki the youngest, sixteen years younger than I, was raised on a cattle ranch in Florida; Lucky went to New York Military Academy in New York State; Nanette and Valerie spent most of their school years in the town of Bergenfield, New Jersey; and I was raised on army posts for the most part. This made for an interesting, diverse family group. I might add that we all have one thing in common—a good sense of humor.

While staying at Uncle Henry's we found, much to our surprise, Aunt Nora was a kleptomaniac. She had her loot stored in the basement on neatly arranged shelves. We were fascinated with the diversity of her treasure. Uncle Henry apparently made monthly trips to the stores to pay for the items she had stolen.

We also found that Aunt Nora sewed money in to the hems of all the drapes. She had a small fortune stashed away in those drapes, and we were tempted to trim them for her, but decided against it.

The next day, we went to the hospital to see what was happening with Mom. She had been moved into an isolation room, and we had to suit up in white coveralls and wear white masks and white hair coverings. We visited Mom for the allotted time three times a day, and since there were five of us plus Aunt Maude, we were putting a strain on their laundry room. That number of outfits came to eighteen a day.

The doctors were attentive to Mom, and she remained heavily sedated. Aunt Maude stayed by her side and was making all the decisions about her care. Mom was worsening, and it looked like she would not be making a recovery. She was losing weight every day. Aunt Maude never left her. We had to come to terms with what was happening. There would be no miracle. We all prayed she would not suffer.

Lucky decided we should get out of the hospital blues and go see a beautiful glacier. We left the hospital in our rental car and never saw the glacier. He managed to get us hopelessly lost, and we drove four hours trying to get to Uncle Henry's. It should have taken ten minutes from the hospital. The good thing is it gave us time together to remember Mom's crazy adventures.

Mom was a fun lady, loved company, feeding folks on the ranch, hunting alligators, herding cattle, having cocktail parties, owning a jewelry store, dress shop, and funeral parlor. She never met a stranger and was even thrown out of a few bars. When she was around there was always laughter and a party. As a family, we were always playing games. A card game or Scrabble could break out at any time, even right after breakfast.

The next day, we were going to have lunch at the hospital. The hospital sat on an incline with a long winding sidewalk to the front of the building. The front had floor to ceiling windows, and the dining room was located behind those windows. We were all laughing at something outrageous that was said, and I was laughing so hard I peed in my pants right in front of the windows. Everyone in the dining room could see me. None of my siblings wanted to take me to Uncle Henry's to change. They wanted to eat lunch. Talk about being embarrassed. Thirty years later, my sisters still talk about the day I peed in my pants in front of the windows at the hospital as if it were yesterday.

It was about time for all of us to get back to our families in our various states and bid Mom a tearful farewell. It was painful to say good-bye. I am sure the laundry room of the hospital was glad to see us leave. There would be eighteen fewer white outfits to wash each day.

Mom passed away three weeks later.

We received the news from an aunt in Birmingham who somehow tracked us down at the Cadillac dealership. We were buying our first Cadillac. I had excused myself from the negotiations, saying my mom was sick and I was worried about her. I was sitting by myself in the lobby with Mom on my mind when Tom came out of the office to tell me Mom had passed away.

Mom was cremated, and she wanted her ashes sprinkled under the big old tree by the little house on the ranch. The tree was old and had the most beautiful trunk with limbs twisting skyward. Aunt Maude would put hanging plants on the limbs of that tree, and it seemed the tree was smiling. The big house was nearby, but she loved the tree by the little house.

Mom's ashes left Anchorage in a box and were mailed to the ranch. She was lost in the mail for weeks. The box had traveled extensively around the country. Vicki finally tracked her down, and she was finally delivered home. Mom loved to travel, and she visited quite a few places in her lifetime. She even traveled after death before she made it to her final destination, so to speak.

Mom was a hoot.

Go Figure…

The Diner on 41

Our dear friend Thelma died from lung cancer. She had given up smoking a few years earlier. We watched her make a remarkable journey. She and Waine have been friends for twenty years, and Tom knew him at work before we became motorcycle buddies. The many fun days we spent together are in our memories.

We went to the funeral, which was well attended. We visited with many of our old friends. Thelma worked with Tom at a government agency, was a motorcycle rider, a real-estate broker, and one of the friendliest, fun-loving people I have known. Party time was her favorite sport. We had their fiftieth wedding anniversary party on our large back porch. The women of the motorcycle group worked to make the party a fun time, providing decorations, cake, food, drinks, and all the rest for a great event. The party didn't end until 2:30 a.m. to give you an idea what dedicated partygoers we were.

It was clear that the minister had never met Thelma. He talked and talked about things that were not pertinent to Thelma's life. She did not have a fear of dying, and she went with dignity, never complaining.

After the social part at the funeral home, we all decided to go for lunch at the diner on Rt. 41. It is a wonderful place to eat, and they are known for their extensive menu. They have the best cakes in the world. Their serving sizes of food are generous and delicious.

We waited awhile in the lobby to be seated. It was well worth the wait. We sat at a long table, filling up a good part of the restaurant on one side by the window.

After having a wonderful lunch, we were ready to leave, and Tom poked me in the arm and said, "Isn't that Will over there?" I looked and sure enough it was Will with his black girlfriend. He had promised my friend, his wife, not to see her again. Will is the husband of one of my best friends, and she had been wondering what this girl looked like. She was average in looks, height, and maybe a little overweight.

I looked over, he saw me looking, and he ducked down so I couldn't see him. It was too late for him. I got up from my chair and headed his way. Will got up to meet me. I told him I would like to meet his girlfriend. He looked very uncomfortable. I went over to the table and introduced myself. I reassured both I would be reporting back to his wife.

They were very tense to say the least. The girl was not very attractive, and she had a slightly crossed eye, which I locked in on. She looked like she hoped the earth would swallow her right then and there.

Before I arrived home to tell my friend what happened, he had called and said he was having his break-up lunch. *Oh, yeah right*. That was the most relaxed break-up lunch I had ever seen. They had been chatting away, with no visible tension.

The amazing part is eventually Will did break up with his girlfriend. My girlfriend and Will are still married to one another. Happily, I am not so sure.

They could have taken a lesson in commitment from Thelma and Waine; they were happily married for fifty years. Some people just don't get it. The word commitment gets lost somewhere.

What a memorable afternoon for me and my beautiful girlfriend.

Go Figure…

A Meeting at Wal-Mart

I had a short list of items to pick up, all unrelated to one another. My best bet to buy these items was to go to Wal-Mart.

The weather was great, the sun was shining, the temperature 65 degrees on a February day and I was looking good in my red sweater.

On the way, I stopped off at an antique store to pick up a wind chime to hang in the opening between the kitchen and living room. After scouring this huge store, I found the perfect one and I needed a hook to hang it. The hook is on my list.

This is one of the super duper Wal-Mart's and when I looked down the aisles, I knew I would be getting the exercise I needed for the day. The place is huge.

The grocery area was the first adventure. I like sugar free Cappuccino and I found it…much to my amazement. I marched all over the area and could not find the pet aisle. After finding an employee, he pointed to the other end of this vast building. I needed a 25 pound box of kitty litter.

On the way, I bought a gold looking watch, bracelet style. It took the saleswomen 10 minutes to get it out of the box. She said, "People don't take it out of the box when stealing; thieves take the box and all". All those safety features are useless. She said, "People steal watches all the time." She was employee number two that helped me.

I made it to the pet section after asking where the nasal spray was located. I had looked up and down the aisle they sent me to, looking for nasal spray and once again they sent me to the area I had searched. Finally, I asked an employee to help me find it. As we were giving up looking, I spotted it on the bottom shelf and it took some doing to get the two boxes of nasal spray out of the shelf. We had to remove product around it to finally get it out. This was employee three.

I was in luck in the Pet Department, the 25 pound box was on an upper shelf and I could jockey it off and plunk it into the basket.

Now it is time to look for a hook for the wind chime. I asked another employee where I would find a hook. He gave me an aisle number but no hooks were to be found in the paint department. I found another person and he helped me find the perfect hook. Now I am beginning to feel I am having a personal relationship with all the employees at Wal-Mart. The hook took two employees to locate it and that made it five.

I forgot to get relish in the food department but figured I am not trekking back to the other end of the store.

I checked out my items and needed assistance getting the kitty litter into the trunk of my car. I was to wait at the front of the store. After what seemed like forever, a young man showed up to help me. He was from Kenya, obtained a green card to go to school and then brought his wife and children here. He intended to go back to Kenya after school but now his family feels like America is home. He was facing a dilemma as to where was home. He had two more years of schooling before he had to cope with his decision. The trunk was loaded and we walked back to the store front together where I bid him a fond farewell. The cashier and the young man from Kenya made the number seven.

There is a table in the furniture department I have been admiring and figured it would be perfect for the spot in our apartment. I measured it for chair height and it was perfect. I asked for assistance in the department and a German lady with a heavy accent was sent to help me. I asked her some questions about how to put the table together and we never did get on the same page. She was calling a bench a table, did not know if the screws to legs were attached and there was no way she could lift the box containing the table. She sent for someone to answer my questions and a tall man showed up who was more knowledgeable. We discussed the size of my car and there was no way it would fit. Now we are up to number 10 employees I have talked to for assistance.

By now I am starving to death and this Wal-Mart has a Mac Donald at the entrance. I ordered something that would fit into my diet plan; a grilled chicken wrap and a cup of coffee. Would you believe it was a bargain and it was delicious.

With the wrap and coffee in hand and I looked around the room for a place to sit. I chose a table with a middle aged black woman sitting alone with her purchases scattered around her. She cleared away her bags and I sat down and the most amazing conversation took place. This just blew me away.

I will call her Ann because I have forgotten her name. I asked Ann if she lived in Roswell and she said she was from Macon. She works for a group that supports deaf children. These children are bussed from Macon to a town north of Roswell for special schooling and it is a two hour journey. There is not a school near Macon that fills these children's needs. Ann starts her day at four in the morning. She and a man pick up the children early and drive to a northern town where they drop the children off at school. Then they drive to Wal-Mart in Roswell and park the bus in the large parking lot. She walks around Wal-Mart to kill time and she now knows most of the employees. She sometimes takes a nap on the bus before going to pick up the children. They also park the bus at North Point Mall and spend the day there strolling around. She told me about the sales going on at the Mall. She had some baby showers to attend and had finished all her shopping.

At the end of the day Ann and the driver drive to the school again, pick up the children and make the two hour journey home with sleeping, tired, deaf children.

I asked her why they didn't stay in that small town and she said it was dangerous to stay there. I couldn't believe what she was saying. It was dangerous to be in a small town in Georgia for a black person. I cannot believe we have not made more progress.

Ann said she has had some brief friendships with people shopping at Wal-Mart. Once, a lady sat down with her at lunch and shared she was selling her house. She had to get rid of all the furniture she owned. Would she like the furniture? Ann said, "I have a friend whose house burned down and she lost everything." The lady offered, "If you will have a truck at my house on Saturday, I will give you a house full of furniture." Ann and a friend borrowed a truck, drove to Roswell, loaded up the furniture and her friend was overjoyed to have a house full of furniture.

This was a chance meeting over a McDonald's sandwich and to think of what an act of kindness she shared with me.

I am glad I chose to sit down with this lady and hear her story. We were together only 20 minutes, the time it takes to eat a chicken wrap and drink a cup of coffee. Here I am writing about this encounter. I was grateful to know there are generous, giving people out there, even if the fear factor still exists in some small towns.

By the way, when I arrived home I measured the space for the table and it was too long. It is good it did not fit in the car.

I talked with 13 people on this outing counting the order taker, Ann and the lady that sold me the wind chime. The day was delightful, everyone was pleasant and the sun was still shinning.

Tom took the kitty litter out of the trunk and all is well.

Go Figure…

The Christmas Party

It was December 17. Christmas Party time! All the shopping was done, gifts wrapped, the tree was up, the house decorated, and I did not want to go to the Christmas Party. I have no idea why, I just did not want to go.

Tom's boss said we had to go because he was the regional sales manager. Okay, that was it. We were going.

I wore a wide-leg pants suit (all the rage at the time), a new girdle (a must at that time), and a pair of dressy sandals. We headed out to a cocktail party and then on to the Christmas Party in Hamtramck, Michigan.

When we arrived, the party was in full swing. The band was terrific. We settled at a table, had a drink, said our hellos, and Tom asked me to dance. We were all around the floor. I spun around, my shoe stuck to the floor, and down I went. I heard my leg break before I dropped. When they lifted my pants leg, they could see I had two knees. My friend, Dorothy, thought I had fainted, and she applied an ice cube to my head. I complained to Tom to get the ice off. I was in the midst of a Christmas Party I would never forget.

The ambulance arrived, and when the paramedics straightened out my leg, I screamed. They put an oxygen mask on me, and two ladies fainted. Off we went to the hospital. I was given pain medicine, thank heavens, and the nurse asked if I would like to slip out of my new girdle. Were they kidding, slip out of a girdle? They finally cut it off at my insistence.

Three days later, after some of the swelling subsided, it was time to set the leg. The nurse was to give me a pain shot and forgot. I was on the way to the elevator when she gave it to me. It had not kicked in when I arrived in the leg-setting room where the doctor worked. I screamed when they lifted my leg. Remember, the two pieces were not connected. The doctor said, "Get her out of here." I can still hear him say it. It was then that I decided he was a good-looking bastard. When the meds kicked in, I went back in to have my leg set. They lifted the broken part as I raised my leg straight up, and I urged them to hurry. They lined up the two pieces, wrapped it with gauze, and then put plaster on the wrapping. The first cast would have a bent knee, the second would be straight, and the third would be below the knee. Mind you, the first two were full leg casts. Each cast would be worn for three months. That meant no baths or showers. How horrific is that?

I was finally sent home before Christmas. Tom had ordered a hospital bed, which was put in the study since our bedroom was upstairs. This was the beginning of some happenings and lessons. Some of the lessons were interesting. When being pushed in a wheelchair, people would stand behind you to talk to the pusher like you weren't present. The good thing was, you would make eye contact with children, and they would talk to you. Sometimes, when going into a store, men would shove their way in front of you. Salespeople would look like they wished you would keep on going. There were not as many wheelchair accessible laws at the time. Things have improved since then. I had a lesson in what handicapped folks had to deal with daily. It was certainly enlightening.

Aunt Maude, from Birmingham, Alabama, came to give me a hand. I was awkward in maneuvering around in the heavy cast. It presented some problems, like getting out of bed. When I dropped the leg down, I would pop right up. One night, my leg fell out of the bed against the wall. I screamed and Tom almost killed himself charging down the steps. Going to the bathroom was awkward; I had to put my leg on a stool to sit down. Once I fell going up the one step to the kitchen. I panicked, thinking I had hurt my leg. Tom reminded me the leg was in no danger since it was encased in plaster. I had no idea how I would get up from the floor. Tom lifted me straight up as soon as I was calmed down.

Aunt Maude believed that the best way to take care of you was to feed you. She cooked up a storm. She would bring me large plates piled high with food. Needless to say, I was gaining weight because I was unable to exercise. I have always had to watch my calorie count. It was not a good thing.

One day I wanted to paint some small paintings. We set up a table by the bed, put oil paint on a pallet, and I was ready to create masterpieces. The cat jumped up on the pallet, jumped on the raised bed, slid down the bed, flew off, and circled the house with oil paint on his feet. Tom caught him finally and tried to clean the cat with turpentine. Did you ever try to clean a cat with turpentine? Tom's scratches eventually healed.

Aunt Maude finally went home. She gets mad at you when you no longer need her.

The moral of the story is: *Do not do anything you do not want to do.*

Obviously, lots of people never forgot this particular party, as I found out years later. I was always bumping in to people that would say, "I remember the day you broke your leg." My instinct told me not to go to this Christmas Party, and I wish I had listened.

Go Figure...

Trees Are Great

We were selling our house and getting it ready for a sale. All the repairs were finished, and we thought we were done. A crew of tree trimmers had been working down the street for a few days. A young man came knocking on our door.

He'd seen the "For Sale" sign on the front lawn and suggested we trim the trees so that you could see the house better. I called my realtor to ask if trimming the trees would be a good idea. He suggested I stay out in the street with the trimmer because they had a tendency to trim them up too far.

I told the young man he had a deal, the price was right, and he had two workers to climb around to do the trimming. They climbed those trees like they were going up stairs.

I stood out in the street with the young man, Bill, and I explained I wanted the trees trimmed like they cut hair these days—nice and shaggy. We discussed each limb, and the climber started cutting. Bill looked at me and said, "You look like you are in pain."

I explained, "I love trees and could not stand it if he was hurting them." He assured me the trees would feel better after they are trimmed and all went well. No tree cried out, so I assume he was right.

The front yard looked wonderful. We had a big hole in the yard, and they chipped up the limbs and filled the hole, solving a problem we had not dealt with.

Bill rang the doorbell; I invited him while I wrote a check. He looked in the living room and dashed in. Hanging over the couch were four tree paintings. He pointed out which limbs he would trim, and the green in the paintings meant more money was coming.

He asked if I would barter, and I said yes. He called his wife to discuss the deal, and she explained to him that they had two children to feed and now was no time to be buying paintings. He was disappointed but understood she had a point.

I wrote the check for the trimming, went into the living room, took down two paintings, and said, "These are yours." The joy I felt at that moment is indescribable. He was beaming. He could not believe they were his, and I was beaming even more.

Knowing that my paintings could bring that much joy was a gift of love. Having had them hanging in my living room for thirteen years, liking them in that room, and then knowing a hard-working tree trimmer was appreciating them…there was nothing better than that.

Remembering the moment still gives me that same feeling of joy. It is great to be blessed. God bless the trees.

Go Figure…

Italy on the Horizon

I was a part of a group of ten artists being organized, if that is possible, to travel to Italy. Wendy was our guide. She made all the arrangements, booking flights, finding a hotel while in Venice, and handling the money. We were counting on being well taken care of on the trip.

Some of us had not met or had not seen each other for some time, so I decided to have a luncheon at my home. It was a lovely gathering, and we enjoyed a meal together. That was the first time I met Cathy. We spent some time discussing how much luggage was acceptable. A small bag should do it with careful planning for the ten-day stay.

We were visiting Venice to attend the bi-annual La Biennale, a contemporary art exhibition. We were excited about attending. Artists from all over the world compete to be in this event every two years. They feature paintings, sculptures, films, conceptual art, and elaborate installations. We would get a feel for the art around the world while enjoying magnificent Venice.

Our plans were to meet at the Atlanta airport, go to the international gate, and we would be on our way. We would land in Paris and have a five-hour delay before boarding the plane for Venice. After arrival, we would take the water taxi to our hotel.

The five-hour delay became a problem. We were so exhausted from the flight, we thought about stretching out on the floor. Someone suggested we rent a room to freshen up in, but we would have to leave the airport, which made us all nervous. By the time we made arrangements to do that, we realized we only had an hour to go. We chucked the idea.

After landing in Venice, it was time to get reacquainted with our luggage. We all had a small bag and a carry-on except Pam, the senior in our group. There she was with two large bags and a hat box. I must explain that Pam is a Southern Lady. She dresses beautifully with jewelry, scarves, matching shoes, jacket, and always a hat. She is always "turned out," as they say in the South. Most of us wore sneakers on the flights, and Pam wore five-inch heels. She is slight, barely weighing in at 110 pounds. Now we had her fifty pounds of luggage to deal with, and Cathy was the only one fit enough to manage it for her.

Off to the water taxi. One was going to charge a humongous amount of money. We were not familiar with the money exchange, and they knew it. Wendy spoke up—she spoke Italian—and we waited for the regular Vaporetto water taxi. We landed at the famous Piazza San Marco (Saint Mark's Square) and almost lost Pam. She still wore her heels, and we had to climb up on to the dock. She slipped, almost sliding between the boat and the dock. I grabbed her arm and swung her up on to the dock. We almost lost her the first minute we touched solid ground in Venice. We walked a few blocks to our hotel in a perfect location. By then, Pam was limping along and Cathy was loaded down with luggage.

At the front desk was the most handsome Italian young man I had ever seen. He was beautiful. I had heard about the Italian men, but this one was breathtaking.

We were assigned our rooms, and wouldn't you know, we had three flights of stairs to drag the luggage up. Pam only had two flights. Poor Cathy, Pam was on the second floor and she was on the fourth. We all just fell into our beds, bone tired. We had a full day planned starting early the next morning.

Our first glimpse of Venice in the light of day was overwhelming. It is so beautiful and quiet. I loved the quiet, no cars, just boats, water, radiant sun light, color everywhere. Just to think, we were going to be there for ten glorious days! We walked all over the city, trying not to get lost. At every turn, there was a beautiful picture. The buildings were all colors, the rich textured walls, cobblestone walkways, the quaint walking bridges across the canals, interesting doors of all colors and trim, open windows with lace curtains blowing in the soft breezes, and pots of flowers everywhere. It was an artist's dream.

We became familiar with the city, tasted wonderful food, drank strong but delicious coffee, ate gelato in all flavors, drank wonderful wine, ate good bread, the best spinach and pastries, and the pizza was out of this world.

The next day we were ready for art at La Biennale. We walked to the entrance, and Wendy took care of the entrance fee. There was much arm swinging and loud talk, but finally we had our tickets.

La Biennale covered an enormous amount of ground. We would have lots of walking to see all the exhibits. They were laid out that one led to another with benches all along the walkways. All I can say is that we had a wonderful experience.

The art was enlightening, original, stimulating, and sometimes puzzling. The one thing I remember the most is a film we saw, and I have written about it. For some reason it has had a lasting impression on me, and I can recall every detail of that film. Installations were interesting, and I was disappointed there were not many paintings. Maybe there were, but I cannot recall any of them.

We had a spaghetti lunch, nourishment for a long day at the exhibits. At one exhibit from Japan, you had to stay in line to enter a medium-sized building painted black. There was one door. We stood in line for what seemed like forever and saw no one go in or come out. The members in the line would change; one person would give up, and another person from somewhere would take their place. I believe the art was about the line waiting to see the exhibit in the black building. What else could it have been? We finally gave up and continued on.

The next day started out with picture taking of our group before everyone looked exhausted. We all lined up on the steps in front of a building. I decided to take pictures as everyone was getting placed. There was much jockeying around, fluffing of hair, tying of shoes, and whatnot. I took five pictures before the grand picture. In my five pictures, I noticed Pam struck a pose in the first one and had not moved in all of them. Now that is a Southern Lady. Everyone else was doing their thing.

We took a three-hour trip to a town to visit a palace and gardens, and when we arrived, the palace was closed. This happened a few times, but the restaurants we found were wonderful and the ride scenic.

In Venice, we visited the well-photographed Basilica di San Marco (Saint Mark's Basilica) which was being renovated on the outside, the Jewish Ghetto of Venice, Peggy Guggenheim Museum and Garden, Gallerie dell'Accademia, Rialto Bridge, and the most wonderful trattorias. It is most difficult to choose what to eat at a trattoria because you want to eat everything.

We went to Padua and visited a huge museum that we could have spent a week in because they covered all the arts. The paintings were outstanding, which doesn't do them justice. Every church in Italy is filled with awe-inspiring work of all kinds. Stained glass, statues, gold trim, painted ceiling with murals, tiles, and carvings.

The water taxi took us to the island of Murano where we enjoyed a glass-blowing demonstration, bought some lovely jewelry, admired the crystal chandeliers, beautifully made bowls, and walked around the display areas. It was a great day. None of us bought a crystal chandelier.

One night, we went to a restaurant around the corner from where we were staying. Wendy had made a reservation. When we arrived, she mentioned Rick Steve's name, and you would not believe the service we received! We also ventured to Harry's Bar, which is a famous bar where all the visiting celebrities go to have a drink. We went to have a drink to see celebrities. No one mentioned they keep the tourists downstairs and the celebrities upstairs. Well, at least we can say we did have a drink at Harry's.

Pam was holding up in her sneakers but seemed awfully cranky. One night, we saw her run. She had not been successful in the bathroom for a couple of days. She got the call when strolling down a walkway, and she tore off faster than an Olympic runner. The next day she wasn't as cranky. Pam had the knack of trying everyone's patience by always being late. We would always be sitting around waiting for Pam. She would arrive calm, cool, collected, and dressed to the hilt. Fortunately, she showed up with sneakers on.

It was nearing the end of our wonderful visit when we heard that Princess Diana had been killed in a car accident in Paris. We were shocked, as was the whole world. Where ever we went that day people were grieving for that beautiful princess. Everyone was talking about what happened, and the TV carried the story night and day.

We arrived home before the funeral, so we were able to watch it on American TV.

Wendy made arrangements for us to be picked up and taken to the airport. Remember, she was the only one that spoke Italian. When the driver picked us up, he thought we were going somewhere other than the airport. We finally realized his error. We had one of the wildest rides by boat to the airport any one could imagine.

Cathy was hauling luggage again. She had been complaining of a cough all during the trip and hauling luggage was not helpful. We all noticed Pam had not put her heels on for the trip home. She was happy with her sneakers.

We boarded the plane, and we were off to the airport in Paris. When arriving in Paris, we realized we only had fifteen minutes to board the plane to Atlanta. Charles de Gaulle Airport is huge! It's just one long building, that had to be a mile, and the bus let us off at the wrong end. We had to race down this long building to our plane. Three of us made it just as they were closing the door. We begged them to wait for the rest of the group, but they would not. They had to wait for the next plane to Atlanta. There was nothing we could do. We settled in for the long trip home.

When arriving home, the men were waiting at the gate for us. Cathy's husband was beside himself because his wife had missed the plane along with Pam and the rest of the group.

The next time I saw Wendy, I shared with her that on that trip, I never knew if I would kill Pam or myself. I did not want to travel with her again.

Over the years, Pam and I became great friends. We share a birthday. She is one of the most remarkable artists I have ever known. She is extremely successful in marketing her work on her sheer talent. She is truly a Southern Lady.

I will always remember the fun we had on our trip to Venice.

Go Figure...

What, the Ballet?

Living in St. Paul, Minnesota, was a different experience. We lived there for six years and experienced snow, ice, wind, snakes in the house, summer bugs, two-month summers, a fall that lasts about three weeks, trees that grow slowly, blue herons, wild life of all types, friendly people, stop signs in the air, and no white cars.

When it was time to move to Atlanta, I was ecstatic. The ballet had a wonderful reputation, and I was looking forward to a new artistic experience. I had gone to football games and baseball games all my married life, and now it was time for us to experience ballet.

We bought season tickets for the ballet and off we went. Tom slept through the first year. The second year he awakened and said, "My word, what are they doing? They are very athletic."

We had been getting mailings to renew our season tickets, and we'd already bought them at the theater. They were in financial trouble and were wasting money on repeat mailings. I suggested Tom take his computer expert with him and see what the trouble was. They found many problems, and management was very appreciative of their advice and recommendations.

Shortly thereafter, Tom retired, and he was doing volunteer work at the ballet. They needed someone who understood business management. They'd fired their manager, and Tom eventually became CEO Business Manager for the ballet. I could not believe the turn of events. He went from baseball to ballet.

He had an opportunity to work with the renowned ballet master of the first order. The two men worked well with each other and became very dear friends.

Tom had gone from sleeping to being totally immersed in ballet. He was in touch by phone with every ballet in the country, getting information so he could run the ballet more efficiently. The ballerinas fell in love with him, leaping and bounding into his arms whenever they had a chance. The Buckhead ladies living in Atlanta support the ballet in many important ways, and Tom became their darling.

It was nice for him to go to work each evening in a tuxedo and see *The Nutcracker* thirty times in the season and make a point not to miss a performance of any of the ballets. The dancers appreciated his devotion.

In talking to the ballet master, I explained I did not know anything about ballet, but I had loved the ballet all my life. He explained that it wasn't important; just enjoy the total experience.

I love the ballet because it revolves around beautiful music, great staging, artistry, grace, and devotion. These dancers give so much and give up a great deal for their art. I will never tire of watching dancers perform. I can watch a ballet over and over again and not tire of it. Ballet is a combination of all the art forms. Who would ever have thought the ballet would become so important in our lives?

Our hearts are always warmed by the memories of this amazing experience.

Go Figure…

Cathy Returns to Italy

It was time to take Cathy back to Italy. Four artists. Donna, a brown-eyed beauty of average height who dressed impeccably; Wendy, the tiny one with lovely gray hair pulled back at the nape of her neck, lovely dainty features, the energy of a dynamo, and the only one of us who spoke Italian. She also understood the money exchange and how to negotiate. Wendy made all the plans, taking very good care of the three of us. Cathy was taller than the rest of us, maybe around five foot ten, brown hair, brown eyes, with a toned, athletic body. She was a very strong woman. She had been diagnosed with lung cancer, thus the reason for the trip. She wanted to visit Italy again and to see where St. Francis lived in Assisi.

We flew from Atlanta to JFK to Florence where we would rent a car and drive to an ancient walled town called Val di Chiana or Civitella. When we arrived at JFK airport, we found the India airline at international and boarded. The flight was to leave around noon. We settled in and waited. The stewardesses wore traditional *I Dream of Jeannie* outfits with green slippers that curled up at the toes. Curry was in the air, strange smoke was coming out of an odd-looking pipe one man was holding, and another male passenger was setting up a small grill to cook. Stewardesses were running around explaining that they could not do that on board the plane. We sat and sat. It appears the departure time was not exact but rather casual, and they were not sure when they would be taking off because some of the passengers had not arrived. We waited three hours, and they finally decided to leave the runway for Florence.

We arrived in Florence and went through customs where they broke all the locks on the luggage. The car was waiting and off we went to Val di Chiana. No one had checked the driving skills and sense of direction of our dear leader Wendy. After what seemed like forever, we ascended a large mountain with a winding road, passing quaint, old, beautiful Italian homes. There was a forest along the way that housed wild boars. Chiana was perched on the top of this mountain.

Val di Chiana was built as a walled city in the twelfth century. The Germans used it as an outpost during the occupation of Italy in WWII since it overlooked a vast valley. You could see several towns below. The buildings were of stone and mortar, square in design, with a large courtyard and several smaller courtyard areas. Courtyards were a blaze of color with flowers and the biggest sunflowers I have ever seen. They looked like they were standing guard over each doorway. The buildings were made up of numerous apartments. At the entrance of Chiana was a large tower that once held a bell. The bell had fallen to the ground in the center of the tower, making it look like an interesting sculpture.

Wendy had met a gentleman named Howard at Chiana during a cultural outing being held on the premises. Asvoldo was the caretaker of Chiana, registered as a national treasure. He rented out apartments for folks that attended a variety of cultural events. Wendy and Howard fell madly in love and were married. Chiana was their special place. Asvoldo was their dear friend.

Cathy had an apartment all by herself. She was on heavy medication and needed a lot of rest in the evening. Her apartment had a balcony overlooking the valley. I enjoyed going to her apartment to watch three villages turn on their streetlights each evening. There must have been twenty cats living in the courtyards, and Cathy made friends with a kitten that would sleep with her each night. She also had a large spider web in the corner with a monster of a spider in it. The spider became another friend.

The rest of us were staying in Asvoldo's mother's apartment. She had passed away the year before. When you walked into the building, you were in a living area that consisted of a large table with benches. The floor was made of huge stone blocks. The fireplace at the end of the room almost filled the whole wall. On one side of the room was the stove, sink, and small refrigerator. The ceiling was held up with huge wooden beams. There was a small winding stairway leading to the upstairs where there was a double bed, daybed, and bathroom. The bathroom had a commode that sat high off the floor. Above was a water tank and you had to pull the chain to flush. The showerhead had two streams of water coming out. Another narrow stairway led to a loft where Wendy would sleep. Donna and I shared this room. I would soon learn that Donna snored. Since I was the senior citizen, I slept in the big bed, and Donna had the smaller bed. We had two windows, one on the side of building, and one in the front. Staying there gave me the feeling that I had stepped back in time and was actually living in the thirteenth century.

After arriving and settling in to our apartment, Asvoldo invited us to have some wine with him in his apartment. Cats were everywhere. One sat in the breadbasket on the table. We watched him cut a loaf of wonderful Italian bread, lift the cat out of the basket, and toss the bread in. He was serving his coveted salami, cutting off one slice at a time and handing a slice to us one at a time. He did the same with the cheese. I found his serving method a little unusual.

The next day, we picked up some food for breakfast at the local store, and we were ready for touring. Tuscany is the place for growing grapes, beautiful, large, juicy, fabulous grapes. The vegetables and fruits that come out of their soil taste like no other. Each town produces their own special wine, and you can't find a bad wine or a bad meal anywhere.

We visited Siena and had lunch in a trattoria located on the huge square where the annual horse race is held. The pottery made locally is beautiful. Donna had a large pot shipped home for her dining room table. Cathy was holding up rather well, but we made sure we stopped often to let her rest. The day outings continued, and we were lost often due to the fact that the country roads have no road signs. Getting lost is not all bad because we saw things no one else has seen on the regular tours. We made it to the cities of Crotone and Arezzo. The churches in Italy are works of wealth and art. They don't understand you can worship in a small plain place.

One day we were off to Assisi, famous for being the home of St. Francis. We drove up a very long, winding road to the top of a mountain. The monastery was located on a cliff overlooking a huge gorge. The parking area was a large stone paved area surrounded by a stone wall, great for sitting on. There were souvenir shops on the tree side. The trees surrounding the monastery are over sixty feet tall, growing up from the bottom of the gorge. The monastery itself was small; we had to bend down to enter the doors. At the back of the building was a large stone patio surrounded by the low stone wall where people sat to rest.

We started out on the walk in the famous forest. The first thing we saw was a sculpture of St. Francis lying on the ground. We took pictures of Cathy lying next to him. Each one of us became overwhelmed with the presence of St. Francis. Looking at those ancient trees, walking the hallowed ground, looking into the deep cavern below, enjoying the nature all around, hearing chanting by male voices coming from the monastery moved me to tears. We all went our own ways on the rest of the walk. We gathered in the back patio, and a group of young teenagers from London were resting in the area. Two young men had guitars with them, and they played Beatles songs while the rest of the group sang. We were having one of the most memorable days of our lives.

We met some of the monks, all handsome young men. We were reluctant to leave, but it was getting late, and it was time to return to Chiana. We found a restaurant that looked interesting on the way. We had a delicious dinner that ended our perfect outing.

Each morning, Cathy and I would sit on the wall by the bell tower and pick figs from the fig tree. If you have never tasted figs fresh from the tree, you must put that on your list of things to do. We talked about life and the joys we find daily. She was reviewing her life in a positive way and preparing to give cancer a good fight.

We all returned home without incident and went back to our daily lives. We were all painting again and Cathy was making pottery.

Cathy's cancer eventually progressed, and Wendy and I became part of her support group. She made the journey with dignity, and when she passed on, we were both relieved for her and saddened. We would miss her. She has been gone for a good many years now. Her laughter, enthusiasm, strength, love of life, love of gardening, and energy is still with me.

Go Figure…

What Were the Questions?

Everyone that has a granddaughter going to college has been asked questions about events that were taking place when they were young. I don't know where the questions are, but I do have the answers, and I believe they would be interesting to anyone that wants to read this saga.

1. During World War II, the population of men went to fight the war and women were filling male roles in factories, where the name Rosie the Riveter came from. At that time, women were raising the children, running the household, handling the money matters, and generally doing it all.

The Victorian mentality of a woman in society was very much alive when I was a child. Basically, a woman married, took care of the home, raised the children, and did the bidding of her mate to serve him well. She had very little input in decisions unless she cleverly manipulated him to think it was his idea.

Over the years, changes occurred when women were given the right to vote, then they were included in the political arena. All of a sudden, women had collective power. They could speak out and were actually heard.

The National Organization of Women, NOW, worked for equal pay in the workplace, equal opportunity, women burned their bras, had rallies, refused to wear makeup, opened their own doors, and managed money matters. They took these changes into their homes, asking for help around the house, sharing cooking duties, entering the workplace in not only secretarial and teaching jobs, but as doctors, managers in companies, salespersons (fields that woman generally left to men). This has been a major change to life in America and has affected every part of life. Women work along with men, children are in day care, men become stay-at-home dads, taking care of the children, and the wife supports the family. Sometimes a household will be moved to where the wife is being relocated.

2. At present, I believe our society has become obsessed with outward appearances, with nose jobs, face-lifts, breast enlargement, diets, bleached or dyed hair, etc. having become commonplace. You can't pick up a magazine without self-help articles, makeup advice; the list goes on and on. Young girls don't seem to know how beautiful they are when they are young. They are at their most beautiful—the healthiest time in their lives. Skincare is important during all stages of life. I personally have creamed my face before going to bed for sixty-five years, and I would urge young people to do the same. Eat healthy, get plenty of rest, and smile at every opportunity.

The inner self is more important than outer self in my opinion. Some families are doing a fabulous job and others are not. Church-oriented families seem to work more with the inner self. They tend to have good communication, decision making, responsibility, and manners. I want to underline that manners are essential. Families that sit down to dinner every night to talk builds a binding sense of family.

3. I personally prefer the natural look, light lipstick or gloss, light power, base, a touch of blush, nails well groomed, feet groomed, sunscreen at all times under your makeup, clean shining hair which is healthy, and a perfume that suits you. Use the same scent all the time. Medicated products are good if you have a skin problem.

The athletic body generally is healthy. A good diet can help you stay a natural weight. Eating fruit, veggies, protein, and complex carbohydrates is a good diet. Limit the sweets.

Piercing today is a way of expressing oneself, and I wish they would find a new way to express themselves. The tattoos of today will not be appreciated twenty years from now. Birth control is a choice. There are many forms to choose from. There are many unwanted, neglected children. I feel a couple has the obligation to have only as many children as they can support.

The Power of Positive Thinking has been one of the most important books in my life. It has taught me to have a positive attitude about life, to see the good in all things, in all people, in all acts of humanness. Love the God within you and keep his or her council.

I formed a belief system as a young child, even though I was being told things I did not believe. I often wonder where all that came from, maybe Divine guidance.

Since I went to twenty-eight different schools growing up, I was not totally connected to a group other than my family. Wherever I went to school, I was usually voted for something but never had a chance to see it to fruition. I only remember a few teachers, and I enjoyed going to school. I believe all of the different people and experiences helped me in later life though.

4. Commercialization has encouraged people to buy constantly whether you need it or not. Young people spend a great deal of money on grooming products, and I think it's

because they feel insecure. Clothing and things will not make you feel secure for long; security about who you are and who you want to be comes from within not from what you buy.

Dear Reader, you can make up the questions now that you have the answers.

Dearest Granddaughter, I hope these answers are helpful.

I love you.

Blessings,

Grandma

The Fortuneteller

The most amazing experiences happen, especially when you are dressed like a Gypsy. The events take twists and turns you are not expecting.

Joining the YMCA to take several exercise classes led to a part-time job offer as Volunteer Coordinator. It was known I had worked for several organizations in that position.

When working for the YMCA, my boss friend Sandy, the director, asked me to dress up as a Gypsy to tell fortunes at the Halloween Party the Y was having. The summer before, I had gone to a women's wellness camp for ten days in the northern part of Minnesota with folks involved with the Y. Sandy knew I read palms but did not do it anymore. She finally pinned me down. We set a time and day to read her palm. We would meet at the dock by the lake. We sat down, dangling our feet in the water. While holding her hand and looking into her palm, I told her she would be receiving a job offer…but, not in California where she was interviewed. She would have an offer in Minnesota. She would accept the new offer and would not have to relocate. It would be a larger responsibility, more money, and a wonderful location.

Her private life was raising a family, working, and maybe a date here and there. She asked if she would meet someone. I said yes, but it would not be in the near future. She would be concentrating on her new position. She would meet someone she has known for a long time.

All that being said, back to my fortuneteller event.

I dressed in what I thought a Gypsy would wear. I wore a scarf around my head, a colorful flared skirt, ruffled white blouse, and all the jewelry I could find. Necklaces, bracelets, large rings, and dangling earrings were to set the stage. They erected a tent with bales of hay. Corn stalks encircled the tent and inside, I had a table with a crystal ball and two chairs opposite each other with dim lighting.

Everyone was in the spirit of Halloween. Costumes, bobbing for apples, various games, ghosts, sound effects, and cobwebs helped everyone get in the Halloween Party mood.

Tom was to sit by the exit of the tent to observe the reactions when folks came out.

People were lining up to see the fortuneteller. The line was long. People were coming in and sitting in the chair across from me. They could ask five questions. I would take their hands in mine and gaze into their palms, telling them their fortunes or answering their questions. Tom reported "I don't know what you are doing in there but the reactions are remarkable... comments like how did she know, whoa, what was that?" and so on.

One handsome, blue-eyed, tall man came in, and I took his hands in mine and told him he was not happy in his private life. He needed to deal with it as soon as possible. He was successful at work and would continue to do a great job. He did a good job raising his children. He should have more fun, relax, and laugh more. His work would expand, and he would find someone to love in the near future. I had never seen this man before.

One man came in with white makeup on his face in a clown costume. A feeling of unease came over me. Later, I told Sandy I thought we had a child sex offender in our Y, and later we came to find out I was correct.

Three months later, Sandy was hired to be the Director of the Minneapolis YMCA. She could make the commute easily from her home. After a year, she traveled to a Regional YMCA Meeting in Virginia where all the directors met every two years. At that meeting was an old friend she had not seen for ten years. They had dinner, and they talked about his divorce. He shared that it went rather well. They walked on the moonlit beach on a starry night until midnight. The next day they met for lunch and dinner. From then on, they were constant companions.

Now, here is the good part.

He was the handsome, blue-eyed man I spoke to as a Gypsy. He listened to my words and shared them with friends. He was a match for the fortune I had told Sandy. He moved to Minnesota and retired. They had a lovely wedding in Minneapolis a year later. All their children blessed them and all were happy for them.

They have been happily married for twenty-four years and are still going strong.

This story never ceases to amaze me.

Go Figure…

Moving Is Complicated

The Lord knows how complicated moving can be. Moving from New Jersey to Michigan, then to Minnesota, and finally Georgia were interesting events.

We moved from New Jersey to Michigan. That move went pretty well. I'd had an extensive hemorrhoid operation. I would have rather stood than sat, so no car ride for me. Tom would drive the two kids—Lisa and John—two cats, and a German shepherd to Michigan. They stopped overnight in the Pocono Mountains to see their favorite performers singing and telling stories. They had seen them the year before on our vacation, and they were delighted to see them again.

They snuck the two cats—Randall and Gwendolyn—the gerbil, and the German shepherd, Amy, into the hotel. On the way in, Lisa spilled all the gerbil food in the hallway. Tom hauled the two cats in their carriers, and John had the German shepherd. He settled everyone in and prepared to go to dinner. The room was on the ground floor overlooking the pool, facing the windows to the dining room. Tom, Lisa, and John went to the dining room and sat by the window. Guess who was looking out the window with the closed drapery draped on her head? You guessed it. There was Amy with her head for all to see. Everyone noticed with snickers, but no one said anything to management.

Once again, Tom hit the road with the carload. Arriving in Michigan early, before the moving van, they checked in to another hotel. The next day the cleaning lady was to clean the room. Tom explained there are two cats, a gerbil, and a German shepherd in the room. She said the cats and gerbil were okay, but a German shepherd, no way. She was not cleaning a damn zoo. Tom cleaned the room, changing sheets, hanging clean towels, and cleaning the bathroom. He walked the dog, fed the cat, emptied kitty litter, and Lisa took care of the gerbil. John was too light for heavy work and too heavy for light work. They stayed for a few days, and Tom was tired of being the cleaning lady, mother, and animal keeper.

I finally flew in from New York after spending a few days with friends recovering from my surgery. I was wined and dined in NYC. Bought new makeup, had my hair done, and was ready for the flight. I arrived in pretty good shape but was still more comfortable standing than sitting. Tom picked me up at the airport, and I have never seen him so glad to see me.

Nine years later, we decided to move from Michigan to Minnesota. Our daughter Laura had recently decided to move to Michigan from Denver with her young son Eric, age three, to be near to us. When we informed her that we were moving to St. Paul, Minnesota, she decided that would be okay. She and Eric would move with us. We were delighted.

We had just redecorated our house, not knowing we were going to move in the near future, and it was lovely. Just the way we always wanted it. We had lots of beige grass cloth, tan carpet, a lovely new couch, and we'd removed the black flocked wallpaper in the foyer. The family room had a huge stone fireplace, new brown carpet, and a white sectional couch, with a new table and four chairs in the corner. The house was comfortable and pretty. Now we had to sell.

A kid from the neighborhood looked through the windows, ran home, and told his mom she would love the house. They came to take a look and bought the house on the first visit. That was the fastest house sale ever, and it made the move so much easier.

We were all ready to make the journey to St. Paul, Minnesota. Tom would pull a van with his car. It contained Laura's household items and a few of our things. I would pull the tri-hull boat, and Laura would pull a trailer with the motorcycle. We were a sight, causing quite a stir with the truckers. They were talking on their CBs, wondering how that old man wound up with the two hot chicks pulling those wonderful toys.

Our two cats, Gwendolyn and Randall, were moving again. Randall rode with Laura and Gwendolyn with Tom. Eric was taking turns riding with each of us. Tom and Laura had an intercom system to keep in touch. I was in the middle, and I was to pay attention to Tom's signals. Tom flashed his lights, signaling we were turning into a rest stop.

At the rest station, all hell broke loose. My Gwendolyn jumped out of Tom's car and went racing into the woods. I screamed, "If you lose my cat, I will never speak to you again!" I think I even mentioned something about a divorce. Laura was keeping an eye on Eric while walking Randall, and Tom was racing around in the woods calling, "Here, kitty, kitty."

I had to go to the ladies' room which was up the hill. As I was coming out, a young woman parked her mom in her wheelchair and ran inside. The wheelchair was not locked, and it took off down the hill. I ran and caught her as she was about to drop down the curb. I pushed her back up the hill, and her daughter had no idea what had just taken place. After telling her what happened, I advised she always put the brake on no matter where she left her mother.

My attention went back to the woods. Tom was coming out with Gwendolyn. He had poked around in the underbrush and grabbed her. I think she'd had enough of the car. Eric was having fun with all the excitement, and I was wishing we were in Minnesota already.

We rented an apartment in St. Paul where we would all live until our house was built. We had a mouse that would make its presence known occasionally, and the two cats entertained themselves chasing it. I always thought cats killed mice. Our cats were being entertained by the other animal living with us.

Boating on the St. Croix River in Minnesota is wonderful with clean air. The sky is always bright with fluffy clouds. We would haul the boat to the river and enjoy the scenery, the eagles nesting high on the cliffs, the beautiful sky, clear water, and friendly boaters.

Eric was going on a boat outing with us for the first time. I explained that he would have to wear a life jacket—it was a rule; he had to wear one to go boating. He declared he would not be wearing a silly life jacket. He had not been to a river or on the water before. Once we got to the marina, he took one look wide-eyed at the river's vastness and said, "I'll take that jacket now." That day he fell in love with boating too.

The house was finally built in the small town of Lake Elmo, and we settled into our own lives. Tom and I settled into our new house in the country. Laura and Eric moved into an apartment not very far from us. She found a good paying job and a nursery school for Eric. We saw them often, and Eric loved to come to Grandma and Grandpa's.

We lived in Minnesota for six long, snowy years. It is a good place to live if you can get used to the short seasons and long cold winters. The best part was the wonderful people, the bright sunshine on the snow, and clean air. After living there for a few seasons, forty degrees felt like a warm spring day.

Go Figure

Our nomad spirit got the best of us again, and this time it was Georgia calling. We moved from Lake Elmo when the snow was piled high. The moving van was covered with ice and snow. I was overjoyed we were moving to the South. I had picked out a house in Roswell, Georgia. The van arrived on time, and the move into the house went well. The moving crew, Tom, and I had lunch on the deck in our shirtsleeves. It was sixty degrees, and we thought it was a hot day.

Randall and Gwendolyn were moving again. Randall curled up on the floor of the car, and Gwendolyn would lie on the backseat with a sheet over her. They were no trouble. They would check out the motel rooms by smelling the perimeter of the room, check out the bathroom by smelling the bathtub, and then look under the bed. When we brought in the kitty litter, they would use it and wait for their dinner. It seemed like they enjoyed the routine of car travel. Going to the vet was a different story though—they would meow their heads off.

As soon as the furniture was in place, the cats started sniffing again. We settled in and invited Laura, Dwight, Eric, and Rachel to come visit. They looked the area over and a year later, they moved to Georgia too.

We have lived in Roswell, Georgia, for twenty-five years, and it's truly home to us. It's hard to remember living anywhere else.

Are we really Southern? We're often asked, "You're not from here are you?" We haven't lived in New Jersey for over forty-three years, but our accents have traveled with us.

Go Figure…

Architecturally Speaking

Entertaining folks when we lived in Farmington Hills, Michigan, was delightful and interesting. Detroit was not that far of a trip from the East Coast. We had family that would visit, and we loved showing the sights in the area.

The city is on the Detroit River, and across the river is Canada. We used to love to say, "We went to dinner in Canada this evening." The Greek town in Detroit was fascinating, and the restaurants were wonderful. There is nothing like a good dinner in a Greek restaurant and walking around in the shops after dinner.

There is a mix of ethnic groups, making for a colorful society. The artists there are progressive, and I enjoyed the art museum. The events they had on the shores of the Detroit River were always festive. We visited downtown on our motorcycle often.

When family members would visit, the first thing I wanted to show them was the Renaissance Center in downtown Detroit. The hotel was a new concept— open atriums, smooth curved lines, nooks to sit in, plants incorporated into the architecture, seventy-three floors above the river; I appreciated the architect's creativity. I was a budding artist at the time. The buildings changed the Detroit skyline in a magnificent way. Looking at the building from the Canadian side at sunset was a sight to remember. I did not realize I was appreciating the talent of John Portman until some years later.

We went to San Diego, California, on business and saw the same hotel architecture. I was informed for the first time John Portman built that complex.

We moved to Atlanta and downtown featured the Hyatt Regency Hotel, another John Portman building, with an impressive twenty-two-story lobby. He built the Peachtree Center Office Building in 1965. At that time, it was the only tall building in Atlanta.

After Tom retired, he became the CEO of the Atlanta Ballet. Many capable women volunteered their time to the ballet. Denise Cohen and Mary Portman were devoted volunteers, along with many other ladies. I met them casually, and at a dinner party, I sat with

Denise Cohen's in-laws. Both folks were charming. I knew Mary was Denise's sister-in-law.

We had an opportunity to hear a lecture by John Portman, and I could not have been more excited. At that lecture, I found out that Denise Cohen and Mary Portman were the daughter and daughter-in-law of John Portman, the architect I had admired all those years. Mary was married to John Portman's son.

While meeting some women for lunch one day, I noticed the building's lobby had artwork John Portman had painted. I related to what he was painting on large canvases. My work was similar, only on a smaller scale.

When visiting St. Simons Island in Georgia, we were driving around looking at the lovely southern homes. We noticed a white cement structure on the beach, overlooking the ocean. We commented that it was blocking the view. Later we found out it was John Portman's summer home, very unique in design. His home has been featured in architectural magazines and design magazines. You can even see the interior on his website.

Well, you are not going to believe this.

My friend John who I have known for twenty-four years invited me to join a Spiritual Living Group. The group was made up of five couples, including John and his wife, Mary. We are all like family, and the Spiritual Living Group is extremely bonded. We have been meeting for five years.

I wound up cruising Facebook on the computer and found Denise Cohen and Mary Portman are dear friends of Mary's. They have been friends for years.

This story began in 1977 and ends in 2011.

Go Figure...

Annie Chang

Beautiful San Diego, a nice Hilton Hotel, a convention in progress, blue skies, sunshine, and a pool by the waterway all set the stage for this story.

While lounging poolside, a doctor came over to talk, and he explained that when he operates, he has quiet music playing, and he uses a gentle touch with little conversation to put his patient at ease. He mentioned he was a very successful surgeon.

I decided to take a tour of San Diego on a Hilton bus. I chose a seat by the window and leaned my head on it to watch the comings and goings in front of the hotel.

Out came a Chinese lady dressed in a Mandarin-style silk, looking stunning. The entourage around her was attentive and obviously appreciative of her beauty.

I looked on, thinking it would be wonderful to get to know her. When she entered the bus, I made eye contact; she asked if she could sit by me, and I was delighted.

She was visiting the convention with a group of businessmen. We talked about the up-and-coming weddings of our daughters. Her daughter was marrying in Beijing and mine was marrying in Rosholt, South Dakota. We continued our discussion over lunch and went on the tour together. Back at the hotel, we bid farewell, but I had no idea farewell was not in our future.

My husband and I were entertaining a group for dinner, and we congregated at the front of the hotel. Lo and behold, in walked Annie with her entourage. We had an opportunity to introduce everyone.

The next day my husband was asked, on the convention floor, who the Chinese lady was. All of them threatened to tell me about her, as if I didn't know who she was. He explained she was a friend of mine. Finally, she found him, and he introduced her to all his staff.

Upon leaving the convention, as we were about to get in the taxi, Annie showed up and gave us all an opportunity to say good-bye.

Some months later, we went to Chicago for a business meeting. We left the hotel and walked around

Chicago. We were hosting a cocktail party at the Museum of Natural History in their huge entrance hall, and before the event, we decided to duck into a hotel to have a drink. Lo and behold, who should be sitting at the bar but Annie Chang? We visited for a little while and then said good-bye once again.

On an occasion to go to Hawaii on vacation, we remembered that Annie Chang lived in Honolulu and decided to give her a call. We made plans for dinner, and she made plans for her driver pick us up at our hotel. The hotel that she owned was two blocks away. She was the first wife of a Chinese man. She explained, once a first wife, always a first wife. It seems he was a successful businessman, and he had a few wives.

It was obvious that the driver she sent us was more than a driver. He was a handsome Hawaiian man who flew a ferry plane between the islands. What a handsome couple they were. He was Hawaiian and very attentive to Annie. We liked him immediately. We had real Chinese food steamed in wooden boxes. We tried dishes we had never eaten before and truly enjoyed the evening.

Annie asked my husband if he would look over her portfolio. He agreed and out came pages and pages. She was extremely wealthy. He asked how she knew so much about buying and selling on the stock market. She'd had an affair with a man who was married to a princess. They met at the stock market every morning and would be together until noon every day.

We did some touring, sightseeing, shopping, eating good fruit, and enjoying the beach. When it was time to leave, we bid Annie farewell once again.

Business took us to Hawaii again, and we stayed in an old grand hotel on the waterfront. We decided not to get in touch with Annie because of time limitations.

We went down to the lobby, and lo and behold there was Annie Chang. Again we went to a party, and there was Annie with the businessmen. How could this keep happening?

She decided I needed a new dress. I was to meet her the next day for a fitting with her seamstress. I wanted an A-line dress, not being svelte. Annie was five feet tall, probably wore a size two, and here I am. They measured my arm, waist, and all the other parts of my body, exclaiming *oohs* and *aahs*. The dress would be green silk. She shipped it some months later to St. Paul, Minnesota, where we lived at the time.

The next day we went to another hotel for a brunch, and sure enough, there was Annie. Who would believe these coincidences? I found out how she stayed size two. She ate a plate of fruit and a cracker at the brunch.

I must mention when the dress arrived in St. Paul it was huge and oh, so green. I never wore it. I sent her thanks and a textural painting.

I never saw Annie Chang again. We kept in touch by mail for some time. Then we lost touch. There must be a lesson in there somewhere.

Where are you, Annie Chang?

Go Figure...

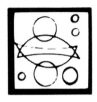

One Day in the Life of a Cat Owner

We have a cat named Pearl, a little sweet, loving eight-pound gray cat. She needed her teeth cleaned and maybe an extraction. They would know better when her teeth were cleaned.

We made an appointment at Pet Humane. They charge according to what you are able to pay, thus avoiding a $550.00 bill we could not afford.

We were told to be there at seven thirty. We allowed plenty of time by getting up at five thirty, having a small breakfast, and making the forty-minute trek to the vet. We arrived at seven, and we sat in the car until the lights went on promptly at 7:30.

Having been the first to arrive at the vet's, we assumed we would be the first on the list for her procedure. Not so. We checked Pearl in, and we went for a much-awaited pecan waffle at our neighborhood Waffle House.

At two, I called to see how Pearl was doing. She had not gone in for the procedure. All I could say was, "OH MY God. That poor girl." We decided to go to the hospital and wait there. We left at three and arrived at three forty-five. Pearl had not had the procedure. We sat down on hard benches to wait.

Across from us was a scraggly little white dog with an amazingly strange hairdo. The man—also scraggly—was holding her, and he had the same hairdo. He proceeded to tell us his life story and how he came to own the dog. Dad had the dog, then the sister, and then he adopted her. The love he expressed for his dog was heartwarming. He told us about where he lived and how he wished he could find a woman that would love him as much as the dog did.

As we sat, there was much coming and going of dogs. They were all cute and well loved. One dog kissed all the dogs that came out of the back. He wanted to play no matter how sick they were or how bandaged they were. These characters were amazing. We laughed frequently at their antics.

One beautiful young woman came in with a dog having a convulsion, and he was rushed to the back for attention. He'd had a bad reaction to the shots he was given earlier in the day. She was shaking so badly I thought she would fall over. She looked as though she was going to collapse. I ran over and held her until she calmed down. She sat down beside us to wait.

Out the doctor came to tell her the dog was fine. She could go in to see him, but he would not be ready to go home for an hour or so. That was one relieved, happy young woman.

My attention turned to Pearl again. She had still not gone in to have her teeth cleaned, and it was getting late. Finally, at four fifteen, she was finished, and now we had to wait until she awakened. At five fifteen, she was fully awake and ready for the trek home. Atlanta's traffic is crazy at that hour of the day, but we made it home safely with Pearl quietly peering out of the carrier.

After arriving home, we opened the door to the carrier and out came a woozy cat. She was wired and she staggered all around the apartment. George, our big twenty-two-pound black and white tuxedo cat hissed; she hissed back and ran around in a floppy manner. She just would not sit down. Her spider beany baby made the trip with her, and George spent some of his time hissing at the toy. It must have smelled like the doctor's office.

I finally rubbed the toy with catnip, and George quieted down. Pearl was still touring the apartment. It looked like she would not be settling down anytime soon.

We put her meds in her food and prayed George wouldn't polish it off; just in case, we stood guard. We went to dinner with some concern, but by now we were starving.

I asked Pearl if she'd ever heard the expression "Cat Nap." She was still going strong, flopping all over the place when we returned from dinner.

Finally, when we all went to bed, she settled under the covers, snuggled up to me, and slept through the night. The cat did not leave me alone for a minute.

When she smiles, you don't even see that two small teeth in the front are missing. We hope this clears up the gingivitis. She will be checked in six months to see if all is well. Hopefully she'll be fine.

The big surprise was that they only charged us $105.00 and that fit into our budget perfectly.

That was one long day in the life of a cat owner.

Go Figure...

Seoul, Korea, and Garlic

I've always enjoyed traveling with Tom on business meetings. These meetings are usually arranged on a tight schedule, and we needed to arrive at our destination on time. We arrived at the Atlanta airport and were to fly directly to Japan, have a three-hour delay, and then continue on to Seoul, Korea. After visiting Korea, we were to fly back to Tokyo, tour Japan (a gift from our friends), and then return home to Atlanta.

On boarding the flight, Tom noticed a crack in the windshield and brought it to the attention of the pilot. We would not be leaving in that plane. We were rerouted to fly into Seattle, spend the night at the airport hotel, and then we would be boarding a flight to Tokyo. They made arrangements for a new flight to Seoul. Since Tom flew often, he always wrote notes to the airline management after receiving good service from the employees. They knew him and were always glad to see him. We were going to be a day late, but at least we were on the way.

If you are wondering how long it takes to fly to Japan for a three-hour layover and then on to Korea, I will tell you. When you have watched two movies, had two meals, taken a nap, and started to feel you will jump out the window…you're half way. It seems as though you are cooped up forever. We were wearing comfortable clothes and doing chair exercises but that didn't help much.

We went through customs after landing in Japan. The plane to Seoul was on time, and we could not wait for this trek to be over. After arriving in Korea, we were met by the businessmen Tom would be working with. He was to have meetings in the morning, and in the afternoon after lunch, we would tour their manufacturing plant.

They picked us up from the airport to take us to the hotel. Our hosts were talking in the car, and Tom asked one man he had not met before what his name was. He turned around and said, "Ho." When he pronounced his name with such a pronounced *h* sound, I got a huge waft of garlic. Everyone in Korea eats loads of garlic. *Ho* is not a name you want to encounter. I thought I would die of garlic smell. We opened the window of the car, but it didn't help. All of Korea smells like garlic. It's in the air. It's eaten in all the dishes they prepare, and it's customary to boil oil in a hibachi pot, drop the garlic cloves in, let them cook, then scoop them out with chopsticks to eat them like peanuts. I have never tasted anything so good. They are delicious with a creamy texture. We ate so many of them we smelled like walking garlic cloves.

Fred, a businessman who worked with Tom, and Sally, his wife, were traveling with us. Fred not only worked with Tom, he and his wife were dear friends. Fred was handsome, had the driest sense of humor, "laid back" became his middle name, and Sally was the classic cutie—perky, slim, with beautiful curly hair.

The next day at the hotel, Sally and I were to meet Joan, the newcomer on the block, for lunch. Joan's husband Dick was a new member at the company, and this was the first time I would be meeting her. I had met Dick on several previous occasions, at a company picnic, once in a bar in New Orleans, and at a dinner. We had invited him to our favorite restaurant, and he declared I would really like his wife. His prediction turned out to be correct; Joan became my nearest and dearest friend, talking on the phone, shopping, attending Weight Watchers and being successful at it together. They moved into our lovely neighborhood, and we became like family. But I'm getting way ahead of myself.

Sally and I were anxious to meet Joan; we didn't know what to expect. Tom, Fred, Sally, and I had taken motorcycle trips together. We told Joan about our trips, especially the one where we drove from Atlanta on a Gold Wing motorcycle to Niagara Falls, across Canada (visiting Toronto, Ottawa, and Montreal), on to Nova Scotia, down Maine, to Pennsylvania, and back home to Atlanta. She wasn't too impressed with these motorcycle ladies. Unfortunately, Sally whipped out some dental floss and proceeded to use it at the table. Joan and I were overwhelmed and left for the ladies' room. I have never seen Sally do that before or since. Talk about nervous! She must have been. Later, Joan shared that she wasn't sure what she was getting into with these two biker ladies.

We three shopped together at the local market. The prices were reasonable, and for some reason, all of a sudden I was the owner of a collection of evening bags. They had knockoff purses, watches, you name it. We were having a wonderful time. Our driver then took us on a short tour of the city.

On this outing, we saw men walking around with puppies in boxes. We learned that they were selling the dogs as food. They believe that white puppies taste better than black or brown puppies. This bothers me every time I think about it. The picture of those poor puppies has stayed in my head for years. Our hosts had thankfully been informed dog meat was totally unacceptable to Americans.

In the afternoon, we were to tour the manufacturing plant, and we were picked up at the hotel. They were in such a hurry, I did not get myself all the way into the car before the driver took off. That was scary; lots of screaming was involved.

After the tour of an efficiently pristine, well-run plant, we went back to the hotel to get ready for the dinner they had planned. We drove up a winding road to the top of a mountain overlooking the city of Seoul. The city was beautiful at night; clear skies and the stars above made the area look like it was enchanted. Lanterns were lighting gardens along the walkways leading to the low buildings. We entered the main building, decorated in the Oriental style of beautiful simplicity. We sat on the floor on cushions in front of a long, low, black lacquered table. This is where we were introduced to the wonderful garlic cloves. The meat, vegetables, noodles, tea, and garlic were delicious. There was a program of five Oriental dances. The women were wearing traditional Oriental kimonos that had been passed down through the centuries. Each kimono had a story. We enjoyed learning the history and meaning behind some of the postures in the dances. What a lovely evening.

The next morning it was time to end our short visit. We said our good-byes with thanks and headed to the airport again. When we arrived at the airport, I noticed the vehicle drove over mirrors that are set in the road for security reasons. It would be easy to see bombs or anything else illegal. I had never seen this type of security. What a great idea.

Our Korean trip was different from the trips many Americans made. I am grateful to have had a chance to see the country under different circumstances.

After arriving in Tokyo, we were met by our friends, the businessmen from the company we were visiting. We were happy to see them. Our host friends were all in attendance. I will save the story of our amazingly wonderful trip to Japan for another time.

Our hosts said, "Mr. Tomsan, you must have been to Korea, you smell like garlic." Yes, we smelled like garlic—really, really garlicky. It was very tasty; I have never tasted better. It took about four days for the smell of garlic to leave us. At last, I could smell my Chanel No. 5 and not the garlic.

Go Figure...

SLG Means Spiritual Living Group

There are five couples that meet at our home on Tuesday nights at seven. We have some wine, iced tea, and a snack at nine. Our cat appears exactly at nine because he is into snacks, too, especially ice cream.

During our gatherings, we discuss a book we have chosen to study. We do a meditation and promise what is talked about stays with the group.

Each one of us takes turns talking about where we've been in our lives the past week. One night when it was my turn, I mentioned I had some major concerns. The next person shared, and when we were finished with our comments, John looked over at me and said, "Renée, what are your concerns?"

The concerns were taking care of the house, not feeling safe with our health issues, the maintenance of the yard, cars, etc. We have a long stairway with a chair lift for my knee, three bedrooms, two baths, a large studio upstairs, dining room, living room, den, kitchen, laundry room, large porch, and a back stairway. Not exactly what we needed at eighty-one.

After expressing my concerns, all hell broke loose. We looked at independent living places and decided The Summit was for us.

We repaired the ceiling in the den, took wallpaper off the master bath and dressing area, replaced wood in the front entrance, replaced attic fans and dishwasher. We began to feel we lived with Julian, our handsome Columbian handyman. He painted the bath and dressing area a lovely shade of blue.

Tim, our dear friend, was our realtor. He posted beautiful pictures of our home and yard. We went out into the cyber world of real estate. The market took a beating in 2010, and we expected to take a loss, but never expected as much of a loss as we got.

I prayed for a young couple with kids to buy the house. The couple had one kid. Each time they came to look at the house, we had to leave, and each time we came home, the top of the urn in the living room would be off the jar and placed on the coffee table. This happened twice.

The next time they came, the urn top was on the kitchen counter in pieces. My burial urn top was ruined. Now I would have to have plastic wrap on my urn. Tom is to sprinkle me under some trees, and I will sprinkle him off the back of a cruise ship.

The motor for the Jacuzzi needed replacing because it had a leak. The company went out of business, and a replacement was not to be found. We finally made a deal with the buyers, and we didn't have to fix the leak.

Next was the garage sale. What a day! Friends came to help me with the sale, and I could not have had a garage sale without them. I hired a friend to help organize and set up the garage sale. When the day came, the driveway was a lovely sight to behold. I have a knack for arranging things. My belongings were going in all directions. Since I am an artist, I sold a lot of paintings to neighborhood folks. It was fun to watch them being carried off in all directions.

We had a couple arrive with the cutest kid, and he said he wanted to buy jewelry for his girlfriend. He was all of six years old. While we were busy with him, his mother and father stole a $60.00 hand-blown beauty of a glass vase. That was the only bummer in the whole garage sale experience. Each day I served lunch to everyone at the garage sale, and at three o'clock, I would serve cookies and ice cream. I made a lot of money that day and fed lots of people.

The things that did not sell went to the Salvation Army. They came with their truck and loaded the stuff and off they went with my treasures.

Now the moving arrangements are to be made. I typed Two Men and a Truck into the computer, and about thirty companies called me to make the move. My family decided it would be easy to move us, and what a job they did. They emptied the house in a few hours and had us settled into The Summit in about six hours—no small feat.

We have a two-bedroom apartment, two baths, lots of closet space, a nice size living room, a small but handy kitchen, large windows, and a balcony. We enjoy the large swimming pool, lobby, dining room, library, exercise classes, concerts, lectures, cards, a writing club, films, study groups, musicals, walking trails, garage parking, and new friends.

We moved in on September 11, which happened to be Grandparents' Day. By the pool, a tent was set up, and a cookout was in progress. There were animals for the grandchildren, games, music, rides, and old people eating hot dogs and hamburgers with all the fixings. That was our first meal at our independent living home. Our family joined in the festivities.

This move happened from March to September. We had the closing on the house and all went well. We did it all in about six months. Who would have guessed this could be accomplished in that amount of time?

Please, John, never, ever ask me again, "What are your concerns?"

Go Figure...

Hi, George

Next door lived a young couple with two daughters: one a lovely ballerina, the older of the two, and one younger, bubbly, friendly, and cute. Their son was the middle child and drop-dead gorgeous. He strived to be an athlete, playing basketball with friends every chance he could. Charlotte the cat lived with them, coming and going during the day. At night she would settle in at home.

Lucifer lived in the neighborhood and roamed around a lot at night. These two cats fell in love. Our neighbor saw them laying around together and figured what had happened, noted the date on her calendar, and three female kittens were born and one male. The girls were white and the boy, George, was a tuxedo cat with a white shirt, white socks, and a mask. He is still the cutest little guy.

We brought him home, and Elizabeth, our grey evening gown cat, welcomed him with open paws.

They became big buddies, and she looked like she was ready to take care of him.

His first night in the house, we settled him in the family room, closed the doors, and went up to bed. You would have thought an army had arrived in the family room. The banging and screaming never let up.

We brought him up to bed, and he played in the covers all night. I decided we would get a cat bed, fill it with beany babies, put them in the bedroom, and sure enough, he settled down and slept all night.

Indoor cats love porches. We had one with the screen going to the floor, and they could watch the feeders for the birds, the birdbath, squirrels, raccoons, chipmunks, dogs, cats, and whatever would appear in our woods. George was walking on the shelf and Elizabeth was walking beneath him. Each cat picked up their feet at the same time and slowly they went, both looking in the same direction. They were following a turtle. We brought the turtle in, and it hissed so bad they ran in all directions.

George kept climbing up the screen, and I spent a lot of time picking him off the top. He picked at the bottom of the screen and out he went one night. We couldn't find him. Tom and I were looking everywhere, and we decided to go out in the car to see if he was in the neighborhood. It later dawned on us that no one finds a cat driving around the neighborhood.

I went to bed crying. How could I live without George? By this time, Elizabeth had passed on and he was my only baby. Tom went downstairs at three in the morning to see if he could find him, and there he was, sitting under a bush. Tom motioned him to come in, holding the door open, and he came running. Tom is my hero.

Another time, George went out the bottom of the screen after picking at it all day. We were watching TV and heard a cat screaming outside. Tom got a pitcher of water and threw it through the screen. The cat was not going away. I realized it was George screaming his head off. He never messed with the screen again; inside is good.

We felt he might be lonely, so I went to PetSmart to pick up another black and white cat. A little grey kitten reached out to me, my heart ached, but she was not black and white. That night I dreamed of a grey kitty and back to PetSmart I went.

George took one look at little Pearl, ran under the bed, and stayed under there for months, only coming out for meals. I would pick up the dust ruffle and say, "She is not going anywhere. If you want to live under the bed, have at it." It took five years for them to have a relationship. We had no idea he wanted to be an only cat.

George will be fifteen in June and after talking to him daily for all those years, he understands English but doesn't speak it. Every time I enter a room, he says, "Hi, Mom." When I ask if he wants a back rub, he flops over. If I ask if he wants to be brushed or have his nails clipped, he is accommodating. He asks to be lifted on to the bed in the computer room; he lines up so I can pick him up. He nags to eat, will groom my hair, and sometimes I have cat spit in my hair. If I don't feel well, he curls up beside me. He knows when I am coming home. If I say, "Get out of here," he takes off. He lovingly stares at me and seems to know where I am at all times and will dig and get under the spread. If you see a lump on our bed, it is George.

We lost Charlotte a long time ago. A hawk carried her away. I never thanked her for having her four little kittens, especially George.

Pearl and George are living happily ever after with a couple that love them with all their hearts.

Cats are great, dogs are too, but we love our cats.

Go Figure...

Bingo Day at The Summit

Yesterday I went to play bingo and bought two bingo cards. I arrived late with a five-dollar bill, and that is a big no-no, only one dollar bills are acceptable. When that was straightened out, I chose my cards and looked around the room and saw that it looked full. There were arms waving in the back; they had an empty seat for me.

I threaded my way through the room and sat down next to a young man. He was helping his mom move into The Summit with his sister and his wife helping. His sister, his wife, and mother were all playing bingo at the table.

Mary won the first game as she always does. I won the second game and later my name was pulled out of the hat for a gift. I was thinking, *nice luck*. I won money, a decorated black box, and a white shawl decorated with blue and green flowers, edged with fringe.

The girl at the end of the table asked if I could push some luck her way; I reached out, concentrated really hard, and pushed her some luck. Would you believe she won the next bingo game? All those at the table were impressed.

Here comes the amazing part.

I asked the sister what her name was; she answered Vicki. I asked what her sister-in-law's name was, and she said Cheryl. The brother's name was Larry.

Would you believe I have a sister named Vicki Cheryl? I told him my sister Vicki Cheryl had a dog named Larry. Everyone stared at me in amazement. They couldn't believe what I was saying, especially since I had pushed them some luck with no effort.

We were having dinner with a couple, and we didn't know her name. I pointed her out to the woman sitting across from me, and she told me her name was Suzzy. Vicki Cheryl's daughter is named Suzzy.

Mind, you all this happened in an hour at bingo.

I can hardly wait for the next bingo game. I wonder if there will be another happening.

Go Figure...

A Borders Adventure

For Christmas we received a gift certificate to buy a book at a bookstore. It was a generous gift from our daughter-in-law Mary and our son Tommy.

On the way to the store, I pictured a parking spot near the front of the store. I was limping along with a sore knee. There was a parking space near the front door waiting for me. Pulling into the spot, I gave thanks, and I was grateful for not having to limp very far.

Much to my surprise, the customer assistance wasn't there anymore. It was replaced by computers located around the store. I headed in the right direction for the book in mind. The computer was there to help you locate anything you needed. I was overwhelmed with the task. Asking a young shopper for assistance was a good idea; she joyfully helped me locate the area the book might be. Not having any luck finding it, I moved to the next book on my list, and another young lady gave me a hand looking for it. No luck a second time. We were not having success finding anything. I found the two shoppers extremely gracious and in full command of their computer skills.

After strolling around, I found a roving employee up to his ears in requests. He had a group of shoppers waiting for assistance. I followed him around and finally it was my turn. He located the books for me with no trouble.

Remembering we could use a new calendar, I looked them over, and I decided not to buy one but use the one I had picked up at the dollar store.

It was time to get in line to check out, and it was a long line winding around the perimeter of the store. The woman behind me had a calendar with Wolf Kahn images. He happens to be one of my favorite artists. Being a Wolf Kahn worshiper, I asked if I could see her calendar. The calendar was beautiful, and I leafed through all the pictures. She mentioned she had tried to copy his work. I explained he worked in pastel, and it was hard to get the effect with paint. I had some luck doing a pastel of his work.

I told her I lived in New Jersey when he was painting in New York City, and if we had met, I would have married him. He was exactly my age, and, reading his biography, he would have been perfect for me. I had seen a picture of him and found him delightfully handsome. She just smiled one of those smiles. You know the smile.

I asked if she was an artist. She said she was a potter. I explained I was an artist, painting in acrylic on canvas. She asked how long I had been painting. I replied hesitantly, "Fifty years." I didn't want her figuring my age, but I had already given that away when I commented Wolf Kahn was my age. The woman standing between us was fascinated with this conversation. I hoped she was thinking I couldn't possibly be that old. She shared she couldn't draw a straight line.

Naturally, the subject of books came up since we were in a bookstore, and she said she hated to buy books because she has so many to donate. I explained that I had just moved and had to get rid of a ton of books. My husband and I recently moved into Huntcliff Summit. They have a wonderful library and would enjoy her donations.

She was amazed. She shared she knew Huntcliff Summit well and asked if I knew Barbara. Barbara happens to be the resident representative, and she recently fell on the ice when we had our ice storm. The fall shattered her shoulder. That is the same Barbara. She told me she was her best friend. She said she took her Christmas dinner. They live in the same subdivision and spend a lot of time together. Next she asked if I knew Bernice, the activities director. I explained I had spent an hour talking to Bernice two days ago about teaching an acrylic painting class. She is also one of her best friends. Can you believe both her friends are executives at Huntcliff Summit? I was amazed at this chance encounter.

I arrived at check-out, and the books amounted to the gift certificate amount. It was perfect. It seems none of the customers were paying for their books; all had gift certificates.

It was a regular day. The sun was shining. I was happily limping along, and it turned out to be the most interesting trip to the bookstore. These happenings never cease to amaze me. I was anxious to share this happening with Barbara and Bernice. When I did, they were impressed with this adventure.

By the way, one of the books I bought was *The Professor and the Madman: A Tale of Murder, Insanity, and the Making of the Oxford English Dictionary*. I enjoyed the book.

How fitting...You might say it "was one for the books."

Go Figure...

About the Author

Renée V. Stark was born in Englewood, New Jersey. She has lived in sixteen states across the country and has traveled to twenty countries around the world.

She married Lee Vining and was widowed as a young mother with two adopted children. Lisa was four and John had just turned one.

Renée then married Thomas H. Stark, and he had two children; Laura was eight and Tommy was five. She had known Tom since confirmation class back when they were thirteen years old. After raising four children, Renée went to college in Michigan and has painted regularly since. Together, she and Tom have lived in New Jersey, Michigan, Minnesota, and

Georgia. Renée feels that Roswell, Georgia, is truly "home" after living in that city for twenty-five years.

After living in Roswell, Renée joined the Heaven Blue Rose Gallery and was active in the Roswell Fine Arts Alliance.

Renée has taught art classes in drawing and water painting. Her favorite medium is acrylics on large canvas.

She set aside her painting to try her hand at writing. This is her first published book. We hope you enjoy it.